Why Swim With the Sharks?

An Unconventional Guide to Early Retirement

Diana Salomaa
and Henry Dembicki

FinePrintPress

First published in 2005

Reprinted in October, 2005

Library and Archives Canada Cataloguing in Publication

Salomaa, Diana R.
    Why swim with the sharks?: an unconventional guide to early retirement/Diana Salomaa and Henry Dembicki.

ISBN 0-9737060-0-7

    1. Early retirement 2. Retirement--Planning 3. Finance, Personal. I. Dembicki, Henry II. Title.

HD7110.S18 2005   332.024'014   C2004-907257-9

FinePrintPress
Edmonton, Alberta

Distributed in Canada by Sandhill Book Marketing, #99 – 1270 Ellis Street, Kelowna, B.C. V1Y 1Z4, Phone 1-800-667-3848, www.sandhillbooks.com

Cover Design by Melanie Eastley, some production!
Printed and bound in Canada by Friesens

To Geoff and Nigel

Contents

Who Should Read This Book?

If you agree with most of the following statements, this book is for you.

- ➢ You want to retire early while you still have your health, and you are still young enough to be active and enjoy life.
- ➢ You have interesting and worthwhile activities you would like to do, if only you had more time.
- ➢ You don't define yourself by your job title and your salary.
- ➢ Your family and friends are important to you.
- ➢ You are willing to forgo the SUV, large house, expensive wine cellar and country club membership in exchange for your financial freedom.
- ➢ You see yourself as a conserver of resources, rather than a consumer.
- ➢ You would be quite happy to live a simple retirement lifestyle, as most of the things you want to do don't cost a lot of money.
- ➢ You are a creative and independent thinker and often question conventional wisdom.

A Word of Caution

We should warn you. After you read this book you may be eager to quit your job right away, and start enjoying life right now. We don't blame you. You'll discover early retirement is a real possibility. It's not just a pleasant, but hopelessly out-of-reach fantasy you daydream about at work.

That's where our word of caution comes in. Before you hand in your letter of resignation it is essential that you do some preparation first. The most important step is to think about the kind of retirement lifestyle you expect to have. Read through this book carefully. It will help you think through the costs of the lifestyle you are aiming for, and the implications for early retirement.

Take the time to fill out the worksheets we have provided. They will help you answer how much money you need, where you will get it from, and how much you need to save. Be aware of the tendency to underestimate expenses and overestimate income.

After honestly and thoroughly assessing your situation, you should be in a good position to know if your early retirement plans are realistic or not. Everyone's situation is different. There are no magic formulas for determining whether you can afford to retire early. This book is a resource that will help you decide. Keep in mind that the ultimate decision is yours.

Part 1

You Can Retire Early

The idea for this book came from our desire to retire early. We are professionals who have spent our careers in research and planning. We have been employed by government and non-profit organizations and have worked as freelance research and writing consultants.

By nature we tend to be skeptical. No doubt this has a lot to do with our professional backgrounds. Over the years we have learned to look for the facts before accepting anything at face value. Something just didn't seem right about most of the retirement advice we read in the mainstream media. It struck us that it was motivated more by self-interest than anything else, and then cleverly disguised as conventional wisdom.

It didn't take us long to discover that most retirement books are one-dimensional. With few exceptions, they focus almost exclusively on wealth accumulation. Winning investment strategies, "can't lose" mutual fund advice, cashing in with gold, making a killing in real estate and other "get rich quick" schemes are outlined and discussed in painstaking detail.

The underlying message is that you need money—and lots of it—in order to be able to afford to retire at all. The experts, of course, would have you believe early retirement is entirely out of the question, at least for the average person with modest savings. Your best bet for retiring early, it seems, is to hope for a generous inheritance, win the lottery, or hit the jackpot with your investments.

Implicit in these books is the need for you to count on your own resources. Retirement experts would have you believe that government and work pension plans will be long gone by the time you need them. In the unlikely event they are still around, the benefits won't amount to much, and will only meet a tiny part of your retirement needs.

We plan on retiring soon, while we're still relatively young, and in our fifties. We're not rich. We only have a modest amount put away in retirement savings. Nor have we stayed at a job long enough to build up a generous pension plan. We suspect our situation isn't all that unique. Many people with dreams of early retirement don't have anywhere near the level of savings they are told they need.

So what is our dream? We both love the outdoors. Once our two teenage boys finish school and leave home, we've often talked about moving to a small town in the BC interior. We want to slow down and have more time to do the things we enjoy, like kayaking, hiking in the mountains, or backcountry skiing. Don't get us wrong. We have no objections to just relaxing either. It's not hard to visualize a crackling fire, a fine glass of vintage homemade wine, curled up for the afternoon with a good book. Or travelling, for that matter. Or any number of other things we never seem to have the time for right now.

Intuitively, we know that getting older doesn't mean we can't still enjoy life and be active. But, then again, why take a chance? We've seen too many people we know, or work with, who have suddenly been stricken by poor health and have had to give up their dreams.

An acquaintance told us a sobering story of what can happen if you wait too long. For years a colleague at work conscientiously saved money towards a once-in-a-lifetime trip around the world when he and his wife retired. Soon after they handed in their notices, his wife died unexpectedly. He ended up cancelling the trip. Needless to say, his heart wasn't in it anymore, and his children got the money.

We want to retire while we still have our youth and our health. Why wait another ten years? There's no telling what the future holds. If we listened to conventional wisdom, it's likely we wouldn't be easing our kayaks into a clear mountain lake on a beautiful Monday morning until well into our 70s.

We don't need a lot of money for the kinds of things we want to do. Certainly not the million dollars the retirement industry says is an absolute must. Conventional advice just didn't make sense.

Common sense will tell you that you don't have to be rich to retire. Take a look around you. How many retired millionaires do you know? How about your parents? We didn't think so.

It may surprise you but the best way to retire early is to ignore conventional thinking. Don't make the mistake of basing your future plans solely on the advice of retirement experts. More often than not their advice is one-sided. That's because it is driven by their self-interest, and it's unlikely their self-interest will coincide with yours. It certainly didn't coincide with ours.

We plan on retiring in the next few years. You can too. Read on. We'll show you how. You won't get motivational stories or investment strategies. What you will get is a practical and common sense guide that will provide you with all the information you need to realistically plan your own early retirement. The good news is that it's not half as hard as you think.

Early retirement is not the impossible dream you've been led to believe. With a bit of planning, self-discipline, trimming your costs, and a modest amount of savings, the average person *can* retire early.

1:

If You Won the Lottery

Have you ever sat at your desk at work daydreaming and plotting your escape from the rat race? You'd love to retire early but don't think you can ever afford to quit. After house payments, car payments, saving for your children's education, and all that routine spending for the necessities of life, you're lucky to find the cash to take a three week vacation now and then. Forget about setting aside anything for retirement.

Not surprisingly, like most people, your retirement savings are nowhere near the million dollars that the retirement industry experts say you need.

Is the thought of early retirement beginning to look more and more like an unattainable fantasy? Is your only hope to tie your retirement dreams to winning the lottery? And considering the 13.5 million odds of hitting the big jackpot, you're beginning to think your early retirement dreams are pleasant, but crazy thoughts, with little chance of ever becoming reality.

Your only alternative, it seems, is to put in thirty years with the company so you can collect your full pension— only twelve more years to go. Let's hope you can hang in there that long.

Wait a minute. There's no need to be so hasty and throw your dreams out. Is early retirement really out of reach for the average person? Certainly, the banks, stockbrokers, mutual fund salesmen and financial advisors on commission would have you think so. But who says they are right?

The truth is you don't need the staggering amount of savings you've been led to believe you do. In fact, the actual amount is well within reach of the average person. You can retire early even if you are earning a modest income. You don't need to be a business executive with a six-figure salary, have rich parents, a large trust fund, own skyrocketing real estate, or win the lottery in order to retire early.

Contrary to prevailing wisdom, you don't have to have started saving in your twenties either. Many early retirees did not start putting any money aside in retirement savings until well into middle age.

Here's A Road Map to Your Dreams

We don't want to disappoint you. If you are looking for "hot" stock market tips or investment strategies to help you finance your retirement dreams, this isn't the book for you. We are not investment experts.

Most of what you will read here is based on common sense. In fact, some things may even seem downright crazy. That's because they go against all the conventional retirement planning advice you have heard over the last twenty years.

But then again, if you stick with retirement industry advice, you stand a good chance of putting in those six, nine or twelve more years at your job.

We will provide you with a dependable road map to help you reach your early retirement dreams. You will discover how to:

> ➢ Make your own retirement rules based on your personal hopes and dreams. The retirement industry uses seven retirement myths that wildly exaggerate how much money you need to save. Embracing these myths will keep you tied to your job far longer than you need to be. Do you know what these seven myths are?

➤ Evaluate your retirement income. Contrary to what you've been led to believe, public pensions can make up over half of your retirement income. You may be pleasantly surprised at how much they are worth. Are you aware of what and how much you are eligible to collect?

➤ Minimize your taxes. A good tax plan is essential to retiring early. Why save more than you need and jeopardize your financial health? Your extra years of scrimping and saving could increase your tax bill and reduce your public pension benefits. Do you understand the tax implications of saving too much money? Are you aware of ways to minimize the taxes payable on your retirement income?

➤ Trim your costs. Most retirement advice ignores costs, concentrating instead on ways to maximize wealth. Common sense will tell you it's far easier to spend less than to earn more. The added bonus is that you have the satisfaction of contributing to a greener world, and still reach your early retirement goal. Do you know where your money goes? Do you know where you can reduce your spending, and still have a comfortable lifestyle?

➤ Live for today so you can enjoy tomorrow. A happy and fulfilling retirement is a lot more than how impressive your investment portfolio is. As a matter of fact, money is probably one of the least important ingredients. Have you thought about what you want to do when you retire?

Are You Ready to Take the Leap?

Don't let the prevailing financial wisdom on retirement stop you from pursuing your dreams. Many people who have retired early find their standard of living has actually gone up. Even though they have a modest income, they are pleasantly surprised to find they have more disposable cash to spend than they did while they were working.

With the right preparation, early retirement doesn't have to be an elusive dream, frustratingly out of reach. Early retirement can easily be something well within your grasp.

Every Day is a Holiday

Imagine not having to wake up to the sound of a jarring alarm clock, fill in timesheets, work to your manager's schedule or meet company goals. Best of all, you don't need to get your vacation request approved. Every day is a holiday. You never have to worry about earning another penny again.

You can get up when you want and do what you want. That's because your time is your own. There is no need to rush.

You can enjoy an unhurried breakfast, linger over the newspaper with a second cup of coffee, take a leisurely walk, pursue new hobbies and interests, travel, or volunteer in your local community, or even abroad. The possibilities are limited only by your imagination.

Can you think of a better way to spend your time, knowing that the major occupation of the day is just enjoying yourself?

2:

Beware the Wealth Management Industry

Take a minute and imagine the future. Old folks wearily plod off to work the morning shift at a fast food restaurant. Retirees bitterly curse their good health as their money runs out, and they're forced to rely on food banks and the goodwill of family and friends to cobble together a meagre existence. Public pension plans dry up, and private pensions disappear altogether.

Not quite the idyllic way you'd pictured your golden years, is it? It's an alarming scenario, and why most people are terrified of ending up penniless in their old age. A recent poll showed that nearly half of Canadians are stressed out worrying if they will ever be able to afford to quit their job and retire.

Luckily, it's easy to avoid this supposedly looming retirement crisis, or so most financial advisors would have us believe. All you have to do is follow their investment advice, and you can retire fabulously wealthy and without a worry.

There's a catch, though. You have to depend entirely on your own savings. Fear is a wonderful incentive to clinch sales, and sell investment products.

While the focus of the industry is on ways to make your money grow, the underlying message is, "You have to be wealthy to retire." Retirement ads paint a tantalizing picture of a carefree, jet setting lifestyle: golfing at five star resorts, shopping in Paris, or sailing along the Mediterranean coast without a care in the world.

All you have to do is hand over your savings, sit back and watch your money grow. It'll be no time before you, too, have built up the kind of wealth you're told you need. Then you can start living the life of the super-rich—and start booking your round the world cruise.

Hold on. Before you grab the phone book and start looking up retirement planners, you need to understand the wealth management industry. Are you aware of how people in this industry make their living from your money?

Run From Most Retirement Financial Advice

Needless to say, what the average person knows about retirement is based on unduly pessimistic and misleading information. The advice you can expect to get in the mainstream media, retirement planning guides, or from most retirement planning seminars direly warns you:

> ➢ To continue working and save, save, save or you'll end up broke and a burden to your family.
> ➢ That you need a staggering amount of money in order to retire. The amount most people have set aside won't be nearly enough.

The following example is typical of the kind of retirement advice you can expect to get from the experts.

Chris and Leslie (not their real names) would like to retire in 2028 when Chris is sixty and Leslie is fifty-eight. Right now they are thirty-five and thirty-three. They both have well-paying government jobs, and together make over $120,000 a year. They wrote in to a financial makeover column in a national newspaper to get some advice on how to achieve their early retirement goal. The advice they got was discouraging. The financial facelift expert, who was a certified financial planner, sternly warned them they would need a nest egg of at least $800,000 in personal savings. This means they will have *to bank over sixteen thousand dollars a year—for the next twenty-five years—if they want to retire early.*

Wait a minute. Let's be realistic here. Who can afford to save sixteen thousand dollars a year—or $1,345 a month—for the next twenty-five years, assuming five percent returns on their investment? It is an intimidating task for anyone, and completely hopeless if you are a young family.

Let's face it. So many other things have a higher financial priority. Buying your first home, getting a car and raising children take a large bite out of most people's income. Where is the extra money supposed to come from to save for your old age after these expenses are deducted from your paycheque each month?

Let's suppose Chris and Leslie ignore the advice they got. They are a resourceful couple and decide to do some calculations on their own. After crunching the numbers, they are thrilled to discover they don't need to save a cent of their own money. That's because most financial advisors typically ignore the significance of work and public pension benefits. The money you get from these two sources can add up fast, significantly reducing how much you need to save to finance your retirement.

In 2028, the year they want to retire, Chris and Leslie stand to get over $45,000 (in today's dollars). All of this will come from Leslie's work pension and Chris's Canada Pension Plan (CPP) benefits.

Even more reassuring is the fact that their income continues to grow, as they get older. Leslie becomes eligible for CPP benefits when she turns sixty, bringing their retirement income to just over fifty thousand dollars (in today's dollars). They also both qualify for Old Age Security Benefits when they turn sixty-five. This brings in another eleven thousand dollars, raising their retirement income to a grand total of sixty thousand dollars (in today's dollars).

Their retirement income could be higher. However, Chris plans on leaving government soon and looking for work in the private sector. This means he won't qualify for government employer pension benefits. But even without these benefits, they can still have a comfortable retirement lifestyle.

With all the money they have coming in, why have Chris and Leslie been told that they need to save so much of their own money for retirement?

It's a good question. The answer becomes clear once you understand the nature of the wealth management industry and the reasons why they provide the advice they do.

Conventional Wisdom Sustains an Industry

Over the last few years, with a huge baby boomer wave set to retire, retirement financial services have come to be big business. For the sake of clarity, we'll refer to retirement financial services as the wealth management industry. This is the term the industry itself has coined. It's an apt one, as they sell the dream of retiring fabulously wealthy to prospective clients.

The wealth management industry includes banks, trust companies, brokerage firms, insurance companies and mutual fund companies. These companies earn profits from managing your hard-earned cash.

If you invest in mutual funds, for example, you can expect to face three kinds of fees:

- ➢ Management fees.
- ➢ Sales or redemption fees.
- ➢ Special fees.

Management Fees

Management fees compensate your mutual fund company for looking after your investments. These fees typically average one percent to two percent—or more—of the total value of your funds. This is money out of your pocket. The fees you pay, and the salaries and bonuses that go to the people who look after your investments, have nothing to do with how well your funds perform! Can you imagine any other business operating this way? These fees are deducted from your account whether or not your mutual fund makes—or loses—money for you. In fact, when markets are down, your mutual fund company is the only one making any money.

Sales or Redemption Fees

Sales or redemption fees are commissions that compensate the broker or other retailer who sells the fund. There are basically two kinds of commissions: upfront sales commissions and redemption fees.

You are charged an upfront sales commission when you buy a front-end fund. Although the rate is negotiable, the commission is typically around four percent at full-service brokers and two percent at discounters. These fees are subtracted from your original investment. Let's say you placed ten thousand dollars in a mutual fund. Assuming a four percent commission, you actually end up with only $9,600 invested in the fund.

Other funds don't charge any commission upfront. However, you are charged a redemption fee if you sell within a certain time—up to nine years. Redemption fees can start at five percent or more. They usually go down the longer you hold the fund.

Some funds may charge both fees, which means you pay an upfront fee when you buy the fund and a redemption fee when you sell it.

Special Fees

Special fees can be a one-time fee to set up an account, an annual administration fee for an RRSP account, or service fees for clients who regularly withdraw money from their funds.

In 2002, Canadian investors collectively paid their mutual fund managers ten billion dollars in fees. Research by Morningstar, a company that tracks the mutual fund industry, showed that between 1998 and the end of 2002 seventy-eight percent of the funds surveyed had raised their fees. Astoundingly, this happened in spite of the fact many funds were losing money.

It would be prudent to keep that in mind the next time you are dealing with a financial advisor whose salary depends on commissions. There is an obvious conflict of interest. The size of your salesman's paycheque depends on the number of investments he can get you to buy.

It's a safe bet you won't get unbiased or well-researched advice. That's because they only promote investment products their company sells, and they earn money from. Most financial advisors have no incentive to tell you about the full range of financial products on the market if they don't earn any fees from these investments. When it's your life savings on the line, it's always a good idea to be skeptical of most of the financial advice you get, especially from a commission-based salesman.

While we don't want to be unduly harsh on the industry, consider this. If you have money invested in the stock market, and your funds are plummeting in value, have you ever wondered why the prevailing wisdom is to hang in there for the long term? Can you think of a good reason for riding it out? Wouldn't it make more sense to cut your losses?

There's nothing more frustrating than watching the value of your investment spiraling down in a freefall. The worst part is having to fork over a hefty management fee to your advisor. Maybe this has a bearing on why you are told to stay in a mutual fund that has lost fifty percent, or more, of its value over the last year or two.

Who Are These People, Anyway?

It wasn't that long ago when only the wealthy could afford the services of a financial planner. Now it seems that everyone has access to a financial planner, or knows someone who can refer them to one. Who are these people, anyway?

Much of the retirement financial advice we get comes from investment advisors, mutual fund salespeople, insurance agents and stockbrokers. Typically, when you are sitting in a bank or mutual fund office, the person giving you advice is a salesman. That's because most people in the profession work on commission. Obviously, the more investment products they sell, the more money they make.

Sure, your advisor may have an embossed business card, an impressive title, framed certificates on the wall, and a nice office. But don't let that fool you. Anyone can call him or herself a financial planner (or advisor). The profession is largely unregulated. All you have to do, it seems, is hang a sign outside your door and get to work.

Out of curiosity, we looked at advertisements for the industry. Disconcertingly, the standards are pretty basic: the completion of high school, previous sales experience, and a high degree of motivation to earn an above average income. A recruitment ad for a well-known investment company sought applicants with entrepreneurial spirit. The job, according to the ad, would allow applicants to realize their *own* financial goals and achieve their full potential. With self-serving goals like these, does this sound like someone you want to trust your life savings with? Or your future retirement plans to?

Likely as not, the person sitting across the desk from you may have been a used car salesman, department store sales clerk, real estate agent, or teacher in their former life. Now don't get us wrong. There is absolutely nothing wrong with these professions. But there is a point to keep in mind. Most people employed in the wealth management profession come from a wide variety of backgrounds. Like your career, their background has little to do with retirement investing.

The scary part is a lot of people employed in the industry are poorly qualified to be giving advice. That's because they have little training, other than an upgrading course or two. Disconcertingly, many have minimal understanding of even the most basic products and services they are selling.

Sales Ability is Important

It is no accident that sales ability is an important qualification for the job. New recruits have to be innovative and aggressive if they want to make a decent living and get ahead financially.

A common sales tactic is to send out brochures in the mail inviting people to attend a retirement planning lecture, or longer-term course held over several nights. At first glance the course seems educational, especially if it is held in your local library or community college.

Don't get fooled. The advice isn't unbiased, even if there is a disclaimer on the course brochure claiming the instructors don't sell any investment products. The next time you receive one of these, take the time to read the fine print. You will probably notice that a "free" private session with the instructor is offered once the course is over.

It seems like a bonus. You get to ask questions and get free advice one-to-one with the instructor. The real reason for the private session, of course, is to build up clientele and sell investment products. This is why the course was held in the first place.

Fee-Only Advisors

In all fairness, before we go any further, we should stop and clear the air. Many financial planners work hard and do their best to provide good service to their clients. There are even some true professionals in the industry. These people are well trained and have years of experience in working in some aspect of the financial world.

For the most part, these professionals are fee-only advisors. How they are compensated is important. Fee-only advisors don't depend on commissions to make a living, as they don't sell any financial products. You pay them solely for their time and expertise. This can either be an hourly rate or a flat fee to prepare a personalized financial plan for you.

It makes you stop and think, doesn't it? Why would anyone go to a commission-based salesman for financial advice anyway? It'd be like asking someone who sells time-share vacation condos for help planning your holidays. Do you really expect them to tell you about cheaper alternatives, like camping? We wouldn't bet on it.

Needless to say, the average investor typically sees a commission-based salesman, and only a select few go to professional financial planners. The reason is pretty simple. They're not cheap. You can expect to pay as much as two hundred dollars an hour or more. At these rates, who can afford them?

We should caution you. Even if you do decide to splurge and use the services of a true financial planner, their overall focus will be on wealth management. The problem is, if you unquestioningly follow their advice you will never be able to retire early.

3:

Ignore the Seven Retirement Myths

Most conventional retirement advice is based on seven myths. If you trustingly follow advice based on these myths, you could end up toiling away at your desk until you are literally carried out of the office feet first. Not a good way to start your retirement, is it?

You're probably familiar with most of these myths. This is especially true if you have read any conventional books on retirement planning, looked at any retirement planning kits prepared by banks or other financial institutions, or attended a retirement planning seminar or two. The seven retirement myths are:

1. You need at least seventy percent of your pre-retirement income.
2. You need a million dollar (or more) nest egg.
3. You're obliged to leave a big inheritance.
4. Don't count on public pensions.
5. Public pensions won't amount to much, and will only meet a tiny part of your retirement needs.
6. You will live to ninety, and therefore have to make your money last for thirty years (or more) of retirement.
7. Retirement planning is complicated so you need an expert to help you.

Myth #1: The Seventy Percent Rule of Thumb

The standard rule of thumb is that you need to replace at least seventy percent of your gross working income when figuring out how much money you need to retire on. We've even seen figures as high as eighty percent cited.

The reality is most people could comfortably retire on far less. That's because the experts routinely overlook a crucial bit of information—your pre-retirement expenses. This omission can seriously play havoc with your retirement planning.

Think about it for a minute. What are your biggest expenses when you are young and starting out? For most people, it's raising a family, buying a house, paying off a car loan, saving for their children's education, and trying to put something aside for retirement. After subtracting these costs, plus all the costs of just going to work, most people would be surprised at how little they are actually living on. The amount that's left is roughly how much money you will need when you're retired.

The reassuring news is that you will still have the same comfortable lifestyle you have right now. And there's an added bonus. You won't have any debt to worry about, or you shouldn't. Many retirees find they actually live better in retirement than they ever did while they were working and pulling in a large paycheque. This is true even if they have a modest retirement income.

Who's Better Off?

In case you think we are exaggerating, let's compare the finances of two couples. The first couple is in their seventies and retired. Their income comes entirely from federal government pension cheques. The other is a professional working couple with children, and they have a six-figure household income. Take a guess at who is better off financially. We think you will be surprised.

Mike and Helen are in their early seventies and have been happily retired for years. They live a comfortable, but modest life, on an income of about $25,000 a year. Mike has never made a lot of money. Given their financial situation, it is no surprise that they haven't been able to save anything for retirement. The fact is, after they paid their bills there was nothing left over at the end of the month. Helen has been a homemaker all her life and raised their three children.

Most people would consider Mike and Helen frugal seniors bravely struggling to get by. Don't let outward appearances deceive you. Despite their modest income, they live surprisingly well on a small budget, and even manage to afford to take a trip abroad every year. Mike and Helen are adept at managing money and stretching their dollars.

Now let's take a look at the other couple, Chris and Leslie, who are professionals and both working. As you recall, we talked about them earlier in Chapter Two. Chris and Leslie together earn $120,000 a year. Most people would naturally assume they have it made. We hate to disappoint you, but think again. In reality, Chris and Leslie are barely keeping their heads above water.

Not convinced? Let's do the math and compare the income and expenses of both couples.

Living Better in Retirement Than Working for a Living

Income and Expenses	Mike/Helen	Chris/Leslie
Income	$25,000	$120,000
Tax/Other Deductions	0	$ 42,000
Mortgage	0	$ 18,000
Car Payments	0	$ 7,000
Childcare	0	$ 10,000
RRSP/RESP	0	$ 10,000
Work Expenses	0	$ 8,000
Available To Live On	$ 25,000	$ 25,000

Chris and Leslie have no shortage of bills to pay. That's not surprising as they are a young couple just starting out. There are mortgage payments, car payments and childcare fees. Not to mention money they are putting aside each month for retirement and their kids' post-secondary education costs. Add to this all the money regularly taken off their paycheques each month for income tax, union dues, pension costs and so on. Together these expenses and deductions add up to a whopping seventy-nine percent of their salary.

By comparison, Mike and Helen have paid off the mortgage on their small bungalow. They have no child raising costs as their children have long since left home. Granted, their retirement income is modest. But they don't pay any income tax, so their $25,000 income is all disposable income. It just needs to cover basic expenses like food, clothing, utilities and home maintenance. No wonder they have money left over to travel abroad every year!

When you take away the costs of working, paying off a home, savings, and childcare costs—all of which they won't have when they are retired—Chris and Leslie are actually living on only twenty-one percent of their working income, or $25,000 a year.

Notice that this is the same disposable income that Mike and Helen have. Despite their six-figure income, Chris and Leslie are actually worse off financially. That's because they have to support a family of four on the same amount of money Mike and Helen have, for the two of them. So why do they need seventy percent of their working income—or $84,000—when they are retired? It doesn't make any sense, does it?

A Standard Figure Doesn't Work

A standard figure of seventy percent is ludicrous, anyway, when you really stop and think about it. It only stands to reason that the amount will vary from person to person, depending on your lifestyle and how good you are at trimming your costs.

Despite what the ads show, we suspect most retirees would be happy to live a relatively modest retirement. We're willing to bet most could easily get by on less than half of their working income. After all, if you haven't been living the lifestyle of the rich and famous while you were working, do you really expect to in retirement?

Inflation Is a Red Herring

Inflation is often used as an argument for convincing people to grossly overestimate how much money they will need. The math can be downright scary. An annual inflation rate of three percent means that something that costs one hundred dollars now will cost about $116 in five years and $134 in ten years.

No one can accurately predict what is going to happen to inflation by the time you retire. So why lose sleep over it? For that matter, no one knows what's going to happen to interest rates, or what the returns on your investments are going to be ten years from now, either. There's no point in needlessly worrying over something you have little control over.

That's not to say we are entirely helpless. The good news is that we can control our expenses. Obviously, it follows that the less you shop, the less you spend, and the less you will be affected by the rising cost of consumer goods and services.

Keep in mind that many of the items measured by the consumer price index won't affect you as a retiree. Or else they are purchases that you can easily cut back on, or do without. The consumer price index includes items like new house prices, home improvements, tuition fees, household furnishings, restaurant meals, clothing, and gasoline.

Unless you plan on buying a new house, extensively renovating your existing home, redecorating, going back to university, buying designer clothing, driving your car a lot, and eating out frequently, inflation will be no big deal. Keep your needs simple. That way you can easily reduce how much you are affected.

We've read that the experts have predicted retired baby boomers will push up the costs of luxury items, like expensive cars and greens fees at exclusive golf and country clubs. With all that retirement cash they've saved—and presumably looking for ways to spend it all— affluent retirees will drive up the demand for these items. Don't worry. If you don't plan on buying a Lexus or golfing at an upscale resort when you are retired, you won't be affected.

That's not to say you will be entirely unscathed by inflation. It would be wise to assume that some costs will go up. This includes property taxes, condominium fees, the cost of utilities and car insurance premiums. Your retirement budget should have enough flexibility to allow for these increases.

Even with unavoidable expenses, you do have some choices. You can downsize and move to a smaller house or to a condominium, or even to a cheaper area. This will reduce your property taxes, utility bills and maintenance costs. You can also keep your utility bills down by being a better consumer. Conserve energy by using your dryer less often, turn off lights, seal drafty doors and windows, and better insulate your home.

As a future retiree you will be happy to know that the federal government is doing their part to keep up with inflation. Canada Pension Plan and Old Age Security benefits are fully indexed to the cost of living. If you have a work pension, and it is indexed as well, pop open the champagne and celebrate. You have little reason to worry.

Discounts for Seniors

We should also point out that seniors are eligible for a bonanza of discounts and benefits. If you plan on doing a lot of travelling, you can save a substantial amount of money on hotel and airfare costs by travelling in the off-season. There are also generous savings on entertainment, recreation, meals, grocery shopping and other consumer items.

These discounts and benefits help take the sting out of getting older. In fact, old age is starting to look downright attractive.

Keep in mind that even without these discounts, you will have the time to shop more wisely and look for bargains. You can also cut out a lot of convenience foods and restaurant meals because you will have the time to cook at home.

Myth #2: You Need a Million Dollars (Or More)

This myth assumes that all of your retirement income will come from the interest on your own personal savings. Let's assume that you have an annual household income of $100,000. Conventional wisdom would say you need seventy percent of this income, or seventy thousand dollars to retire on.

A five percent rate of return on your investment means you would have to save $1.4 million dollars to see a return of seventy thousand dollars a year. A sobering thought, isn't it? How close are you to your million dollars?

If you have a ten percent rate of return you only need to save $700,000. Before you get too excited, do you know of any investments that will generate ten percent returns over the next ten, twenty or thirty years? If you do, please let us know about them.

What happens if you can only get a three percent return? Even this looks pretty good when you think about the recent freefall in the value of your mutual funds. You will need to have $2.3 million dollars in savings!

Do you feel discouraged? Tempted to give up on your early retirement plans altogether?

The wealth management industry has discovered that the million-dollar savings myth is a brilliant sales strategy. They have successfully used it to:

- ➢ Panic people into saving for retirement. Ads admonish us it's never too soon to start saving, no matter what your circumstances, or how young you are.
- ➢ Convince people they have to put their money into riskier investments like mutual funds. Your chances of retiring early are completely hopeless unless you do.

Let's take a closer look at these two assumptions.

Save Even If You Are Young Or In Debt

Retirement planning guides admonish people to start saving for retirement as soon as they are old enough to get their first paycheque. Don't panic or feel guilty if you haven't put the money from your first paper route or babysitting job into a Registered Retirement Savings Plan (RRSP).

Besides, what young person is thinking about retirement? For their sake we hope they aren't. Personally, we think young adults would be far better off travelling, working overseas, having fun, and generally just experiencing life before they think about retirement.

In fact, there is something disconcerting about seeing young people diligently saving any extra money they have for their old age. When do they plan on having a life? If they wait too long, it may never happen.

The reality is that most young adults can't afford to save for their retirement anyway. At this stage of their life they are establishing themselves in their careers, getting married and starting a family.

It makes a lot more sense to pay off the mortgage on their house, get rid of any debts, and save for their children's education first. Ideally, most people will have met these obligations by middle age. This still gives most people plenty of time to start saving for retirement.

If you control your spending, there is no reason why you shouldn't be able to put aside enough money to build up a comfortable nest egg by your mid fifties. Keep in mind that you don't need a million dollars, or anything close to it, in order to retire. If you're lucky enough to work somewhere that has a decent company pension plan, you may not need to put anything aside in RRSPs at all.

Put Your Money Into Higher Return Investments

Few people actually expect to save a million dollars. The trick is to put the money you do save to work so it can grow on its own. This is no easy task. If you go the safe route, going for low risk investments like GICs, term deposits and Canada Savings Bonds, you're looking at lower rates of returns.

For example, a three percent interest rate on your savings will take over twenty-three years to double your money. If you can get a ten percent return you can double your money in just over seven years. There is a catch, though. You have to put your money into riskier investments, like mutual funds to get that higher return. That's because you trade off security and guaranteed returns for the hope your money will grow faster. This helps explain why many people are willing to gamble with their savings. It's the only way they think they can ever hope to reach their retirement savings goal.

Mind you, winning the lottery or inheriting your wealthy aunt's millions are other ways some people hope to put together their retirement nest egg. These are about as sure a bet as hitting the jackpot in the stock market. Don't count on them as a way to finance your retirement, just as you shouldn't count on big returns on your investments to finance your retirement either.

Consequences of Jumping on the Bandwagon
We don't want to leave you with the wrong impression. There is absolutely nothing wrong with wanting high returns on your investments. Who wouldn't? The problem is that an investment strategy that depends on high returns is risky. You might not get any return at all. Even worse, you could lose part—or even all—of your initial investment.

Sure, you can research investments to reduce possible risks. But let's face it, who has the time? There is a steep learning curve if you want to stay on top of things. You have to read extensively to understand market conditions, research company portfolios, and watch the stock markets on a daily basis. Market timing is important. You need to know what to buy and when to sell.

The cost of failure is high. If you make the wrong choices, your plans of making a healthy return can vanish, along with your dreams of early retirement. After a busy day at the office, fighting traffic, making dinner, driving kids to music lessons, catching up on laundry, and all the other mundane chores that need to be done, who feels like managing an investment portfolio? Do you really need the added stress?

Not surprisingly, most people opt for easier solutions. They make investment decisions based on what's "hot" today, get a "can't lose" tip from a friend or colleague, or depend on their sales-commissioned financial advisor for advice. While these are relatively easy options, they are dicey ways to manage your early retirement plans.

Remember the technology and telecommunications stocks and funds? As if anyone can forget, especially if you were one of the unfortunate investors who lost their shirt. As you may recall, at one time these were the hottest investments on the market, and were recommended by advisors. If it's any consolation, you weren't alone in jumping on the bandwagon. Everyone was clamoring to get a piece of the action. In retrospect, who had any idea these stocks were so dangerously overvalued?

The bad news is if you were one of the investors near retirement age who lost heavily, you may never recoup your losses. It has been estimated that if you lost forty percent of the value of your investments, it will take eight years just to get your initial investment back. That's optimistically assuming a growth rate of 6.5%.

If you lost seventy percent of your investment, you will probably never get your money back. It will take at least twenty years to get back to where you started, again assuming a 6.5% return on your investment. If your return is less, it will take even longer. The problem is that if you are nearing retirement age, you don't have the luxury of waiting that long. You need the money soon.

Safe Investments Are Under-rated

Personally we would rather be out skiing—or doing almost anything else for that matter—than spending a lot of time poring over dull company annual reports and financial statements written in dry legalese. Who needs the stress? Besides, we value our sleep too much.

Why lie awake at night worrying about the unpredictability of the stock market? That's why we have opted for safe investments like government bonds and guaranteed investment certificates to build up our retirement nest egg.

We were pleased to know that our conservative investment strategy was a clever move after all. A recent study by Bruce Cohen, an industry financial analyst and writer, compares the performance of various investments over a five-year time period.

Average Annual Returns of Various Investments
June 30, 1998 – June 30, 2003

Type of Investment	Average Return
Canada Savings Bonds Canada Premium Bonds	5.2%
Toronto Stock Exchange Composite Index Fund	0.5%
Average Canadian Equity Mutual Fund	1.5%
Average Bond Fund	4.3 – 4.9%
Average Money Market Fund	3.2%

Like us, if you purchased a savings bond in 1998, you enjoyed a compound annual return of just over five percent. Of course, most financial advisors would view you as a rank amateur when it comes to investing.

Console yourself with the fact you have the last laugh. The average fund on the Toronto Stock Exchange composite index only earned 0.5% and the average Canadian equity mutual fund earned 1.5% in this time period. You are not really such a hopelessly unsophisticated rube after all. Go ahead. Give yourself a well-deserved pat on the back. Your conservative investment outperformed the other investments shown for that time period.

It is easy to blame these dismal returns on the bear market. After all, the experts will be quick to tell you, it is only a short-term blip until the markets rebound. You might want to think again. The study found that savings bonds also perform well over the longer term. In the last fifteen years, Canada Savings Bonds and Canada Premium Bonds outperformed the same market investments described earlier more than sixty percent of the time, as long as the bond was held to maturity and reinvested in a new issue.

This study reinforces our conservative investment strategy. More importantly, we are secure in the knowledge that our money is slowly, but steadily growing. We're not stressed out thinking we could lose it all. These days a four percent or five percent rate of return looks pretty good. It is even more attractive when you compare it to the huge losses many investors have faced when the stock market crashed—along with their dreams.

The point is, if you realize you don't need a large sum of money to retire, you can easily and steadily build up your nest egg with a lower rate of return. The advantage, of course, is there is little risk to your principal.

It astonishes us the number of people who are counting on ten percent returns—or even higher—on their investments. Anything less, they say, and they can't afford to retire early.

A much better way to reach your goal is to cut back your spending and adopt a simpler lifestyle. Not only is this an easier solution, your personal spending is something you can control. The stock market is volatile. Why take a chance and gamble away your dreams?

Myth #3: You're Obliged to Leave a Big Inheritance

Retirement planners automatically assume you plan on leaving a big estate in your will. Conventional retirement wisdom dictates that you will live off the interest your investment generates. Your grateful relatives get the original investment when you die.

While it's nice to take care of your family and friends financially, the downside, of course, is that you have to save more.

Have you ever thought that the whole concept of inheritance is crazy? Why should we expect to get a windfall when our parents die? By the same token, why do we need to leave one for our children?

Personally, we don't think there is anything wrong with spending and enjoying every last cent—and leaving absolutely nothing behind. As Stephen Pollan in his bestseller *Die Broke* puts it, every penny left unspent after you die is a failing. In fact, he advises that the last cheque you write should be to your undertaker. And it should bounce.

Of course, we are not actually suggesting you carry things this far. The kids would probably appreciate it if you spring for the cash to pay for your own burial or cremation. It's bad enough they don't get anything.

Now don't get us wrong. We are not really as callous as we sound. It just strikes us that there is a better way to help out your children, or whoever you decide to leave your fortune to. Instead of worrying about preserving a big pile of money for the reading of the will, why not help your children out while you are still alive?

The benefit of this approach is fairly obvious. You will have the joy and satisfaction of being thanked personally. Surely this is better than having your children pat your coffin, no doubt with tears of gratitude in their eyes, as it is being lowered into the ground.

Besides, don't you think that it is silly to have an eighty-five-year old hoarding a pile of cash so that she can give it away to her sixty-year old "kids" when she dies? Most kids can use the cash when they are young. Why make them wait until they are senior citizens themselves? At that point, they probably don't need the money anymore, anyway.

The advantage of the *Die Broke* approach is that early retirement becomes a real possibility. Obviously, that's because you don't have to save nearly as much money. There is no need for a large pool of capital to generate interest income to finance your retirement, or to provide a generous inheritance.

Family Squabbles

Family lawyers will also be quick to tell you that leaving a large inheritance has its drawbacks. They should know, having witnessed first-hand plenty of "knock down and drag them out fights" in court over the division of family assets. It would be enough to disillusion anyone about the strength of family ties. They know from bitter experience that sibling rivalry doesn't always go away with age, hindsight and maturity.

Vacation property often seems to create the most headaches, as well as some correspondingly absurd advice handed out by estate planners. Elderly couples are routinely advised to buy extra insurance if they don't have a lot of assets for the kids, other than the family cottage. The reasoning goes like this. One sibling keeps the cottage and the other kids divide the insurance bonanza. Presumably this will make everyone happy. We weren't so sure about the parents, though. They are the ones left paying the insurance premiums.

We recently saw a variation of this advice on TV ads by a well-known insurance company. The agent urges the parents to buy an insurance policy to pay off any capital gains on their house and cottage. This time the kids pay the premiums! Naturally, insurance companies want to get in on the action.

Time of Reckoning

Aside from saving more than you need, and the ensuing family bickering over the division of your estate, there is another practical reason for not worrying about leaving an inheritance for the kids. Be aware that you will eventually have to cash in your registered tax sheltered savings plans and pay income tax on your withdrawals. There is a definite shortcoming to all this extra money. You will find yourself bumped up into a higher tax bracket faster than you can say RRSP.

You may start wondering whether your years of scrimping and saving were worth it. Maybe you should have spent some of your savings instead, had fun and enjoyed your money while you were young. If you had to do it all over again, what would you rather do? Ocean kayak for a month in the Salomon Islands? Cycle through vineyards and quaint villages in Provence? Visit art galleries in Europe? Or, write out quarterly cheques to the federal government in your old age? In hindsight, the answer seems fairly obvious, doesn't it?

Don't expect the folks over at Revenue Canada to appreciate your years of virtuous self-sacrifice, or feel sorry for you. On the contrary, they'll thank you for your diligence. The fact is the federal government can hardly wait to cash in on the tax bonanza as affluent boomers age and start cashing in their RRSPs.

Myth #4: Don't Count on Public Pensions

As a future senior-to-be in Canada it is heartening to know that you can count on drawing benefits from the

Canada Pension Plan (CPP) as early as age sixty, and from the Old Age Security (OAS) program when you turn sixty-five.

Yet, conventional wisdom would have you believe that you are hopelessly green and misguided if you are counting on Ottawa to take care of you in your old age. Retirement experts will be quick to warn you that your golden years won't be nearly as golden as you are expecting if you go this route.

Canada Pension Plan (CPP)

The wealth management industry would have you believe that the Canada Pension Plan is dangerously underfunded. Aside from their obvious self-interest, the rationale for this line of thinking is fairly straightforward. The industry assumes there will be a taxpayer revolt, as young people will refuse to pay skyrocketing taxes. After all, why should they support a large wave of retired boomers cashing in government pension cheques—while they trudge off to work to pay for it all?

In reality, the picture isn't nearly as gloomy as financial advisors would have you think. Politicians realized the Canada Pension Plan was headed for trouble in the mid 1990's. They made some bold changes to the plan to defuse this demographic time bomb—still ticking away, by the way, in the United States and many European countries that are also faced with a rapidly aging population.

The first reform made by the federal government was to nearly double the compulsory contribution rate. Prior to 1998 the rate was 6.6% of eligible earnings. By 2003 it went up to 9.9% of eligible earnings, where it is expected to stay.

With all the extra cash pouring in, CPP contributions to the plan are expected to exceed benefit payments until 2021. This extra money can be invested for the next sixteen years, and will build up a healthy pool of capital. Reassuringly, the last review of the plan by the chief actuary of Canada concluded the CPP will collect enough money through premiums and investment income to meet its obligations until at least 2075.

There's no reason why you shouldn't count on this money in your old age. John MacNaughton, the recent president and CEO of the Canada Pension Plan Investment Board, certainly has no doubts about the plan's viability. He has stated in public meetings throughout Canada that the Board has every confidence the plan is sustainable.

The other major change made by the federal government was to modify how CPP monies are managed. Legislation was passed to ensure funds in the plan are held at arm's length from government. This was done through the creation of the CPP Investment Board. The Board's task is much like a custodian. Their job is to keep our retirement money in safekeeping and invest it on our behalf until it is needed to pay out benefits.

Because Canada's CPP fund is now kept in a separate account, it is harder to raid by governments of the day. It is not part of the big pot of cash the federal government routinely relies on to pay for ongoing programs and general expenses.

If the federal government wanted to loot the piggy bank, and use this money for something else, they would have to get agreement from provinces representing two-thirds of the population, with the exception of Quebec as it runs its own plan. Can you think of anything the federal government and the provinces have agreed on lately? There are times when political grandstanding, constitutional squabbles and the slow pace of bureaucracy can be downright reassuring.

This is a far cry from the situation in the United States, where they are still sitting on a ticking time bomb. Money to fund the retirement needs of boomers comes out of the United States government's social security account. This makes it easy to raid in order to finance other pet projects, or to offer election goodies, like tax cuts. In fact, this account has been looted so frequently that there is speculation that by 2016, when boomers start retiring in big numbers in the United States, the pot may run dry.

If the U.S. government doesn't have enough money to pay their pensions, they will have to borrow it. This will have repercussions on future retirees. There will be pressure to reduce pension benefits, have workers make bigger contributions, or raise the retirement age, all of which are worrying options.

Old Age Security (OAS)

The federal government's Old Age Security program is a little more vulnerable to the whims of finance ministers. That's because it is an income program funded through general tax revenues, rather than contributions from individuals.

There have been several attempts over the years to tinker with the program. For example, there was a move to pay out benefits on the basis of joint family income, rather than on each person's net individual income, the way it works now.

The thinking behind proposed changes to the OAS program was that baby boomers would take advantage of RRSP contributions, and save for their own retirement. Politicians were naively hoping the OAS program would not be needed anymore.

Reality usually bears little resemblance to wishful thinking. It turns out most Canadians are using any spare cash they have to buy a house, go to school, or pay for their children's education. There isn't much left over to put into an RRSP.

Fortunately, seniors are a feisty bunch. The federal government has discovered this, to their consternation, every time they have tried to modify the OAS program. Seniors have the time to organize and lobby against any proposals to change their benefits, with the result the government has had to quickly back down.

Their political clout can be expected to grow, thanks to the sheer number of aging baby boomers. It will be a tough battle to get rid of the OAS program, or change how benefits are paid out. What senior, or person approaching retirement, for that matter, would support any politician or political party that tried?

If it's any reassurance, the administrator of the OAS program, the federal Department of Social Development, has repeatedly stated that OAS costs are affordable. Moreover, they say OAS cheques will be there for you when you need them.

Granted, there is no guarantee that future governments won't try means testing or other ways to pare down this huge expenditure when times get rough. There is no point worrying about it, though. Ballot boxes are a powerful tool. It's reassuring to know that you can vote out any politician who tries to tamper with your benefits. Given that many people have few retirement savings, it only stands to reason that most retirees, and soon-to-be retirees, are unlikely to support a political party that tries to reduce their retirement income.

Myth #5: Public Benefits Won't Amount to Much

Naturally, because of the previous myth, a common mistake people make when calculating their retirement income is to forget about federal government pension benefits. Don't make this mistake. The amounts you are entitled to can be substantial.

A single person who retires at age sixty-five could receive fifteen thousand dollars a year from government sources alone, or about $1,250 a month, at the time of writing. This assumes they get the average CPP benefit, don't have a company pension plan, and have no registered retirement savings. They are entitled to extra OAS benefits because their retirement income is modest.

A couple could get almost $25,500 a year—or over $2,100 a month in government benefits alone. Again, keep in mind this assumes they have both worked, retire at age sixty-five, and receive the average CPP payment and their maximum OAS benefits.

Many couples enjoy a comfortable retirement on public pensions alone. This is especially true if they live a simple lifestyle, own their own house, and are debt-free. Mind you, if you can't live without the expensive holidays and wardrobe full of designer clothes, you will have to top up your public benefits with a substantial amount of your own money.

It is a little different if you are single. In that case, you will need some personal savings, as your government cheques likely won't be enough. As you can see though, a steady stream of government pension benefits means that you can drastically cut back the amount of money you have to save.

Myth #6: You'll Live to Ninety

Most financial advisors automatically assume your money has to last for at least thirty years once you retire. Obviously that's because we are all going to live to ninety.

We read about a fifty-year old businesswoman who was told she had to save enough money to last until she is a hundred. The absurdity of this advice really hits home when you find out she has cancer. No doubt this advice is reassuring, considering her medical condition, but the reality isn't nearly as optimistic. Even though her disease is currently in remission, there's only an outside chance, at best, she'll live another fifty years—even if she were in the best of health.

It is comforting to believe that medical research will wipe out many diseases in our lifetime. Certainly this is what the wealth management industry would have us believe, at any rate. That's because if you expect to live to a ripe old age you have to save more—and invest more. After all, who wants to risk outliving their assets and ending up broke in their old age?

A trusting belief in longevity—especially their own—makes most people complacent. It's easy to get a false sense of security. There's no need to stop and smell the roses. Why feel guilty about your frenzied pace of life, or re-evaluate your priorities, if you can have it all? There will be plenty of time to slow down, take care of your health, and start enjoying life when you retire. You've got at least thirty years, right?

Sorry, we hate to disillusion you. But health statistics paint an entirely different picture. And the numbers are not reassuring.

Even with the advances in modern medicine, the average life span in Canada is seventy-seven for men and eighty-two for women. If you are a male and retire at sixty-five you might have another twelve years left to enjoy the rest of your life.

Sobering thought, isn't it? Think of how fast the last decade went by.

The average female can look forward to enjoying about seventeen years of retirement, assuming she retires at sixty-five.

Quality of Life

The numbers are even more discouraging if you take quality of life into consideration. This is how many years of good health the average person can expect to have from birth.

The average male can look forward to his sixty-seventh birthday before any significant health problems limit his mobility. The age is around seventy for women.

Most Canadian men will enjoy two years of good health, on average, if they retire at sixty-five. The figure is five for women. This means most retirees will be spending a good part of their "golden years" sitting in a doctor's office or in their easy chair at home. That's because they will be coping with high blood pressure, arthritis, heart disease, prostate cancer, or some other disability that limits their physical activity.

Mind you, these are statistical averages. If you look after your health now, there is no reason why you can't beat the odds and look forward to a long and healthy retirement. Who knows? You could be one of the people that we occasionally read about who are running marathons in their seventies.

Be forewarned, though. This won't happen if you don't take an active role in your health, starting right now. The fact is most people take their health for granted. Health statistics show that less than half of Canadian men and women over the age of twelve consider themselves active, or even moderately active.

This is not a good start to retirement—or the rest of your life, for that matter.

Wealth and Fame Aren't Much Help
Wealth or fame is no guarantee of a long life, either. Just look at some of the famous people who had it all and died at a relatively young age.

Famous People Who Have Died Young

Famous Person	Died	Occupation
Stevie Ray Vaughn	35	Blues Guitarist
John Denver	53	Singer
Toni Onley	75	Artist
Margaret Laurence	60	Author
Gianni Versace	50	Fashion Designer
Audrey Hepburn	63	Actress
Stan Rogers	33	Folk Singer
Robert Atkins	72	Lifestyle Guru
Charles Schulz	77	Cartoonist
Dian Fossey	53	Primatologist
Jacqueline Kennedy Onassis	65	First Lady
Stanley Kubrick	70	Film Director
Warren Zevon	56	Singer
Barbara Frum	54	Journalist
Charles Mingus	56	Jazz Bassist
Jim Croce	30	Singer

Makes you stop and think, doesn't it? What's the point of putting in long hours, working hard and coming home exhausted? The sacrifices you are making aren't worth it, as you probably don't need all that money for your retirement, anyway.

Don't you think it is time we got our priorities straight? Life is short. We don't have nearly as long as we think we do. How much longer do you want to stay in the rat race? There's a lot of built-in stress when you're intent on climbing your way to the top: five days vacation a year, working overtime and weekends, heading off to the office at seven, long hours commuting, wolfing down a quick sandwich at your desk.

You're neglecting your friends and family for your job. Are the fast pace, anxiety, and personal sacrifices you're making worth it?

Don't make the mistake of putting off your dreams too long. Worse, don't trade in your dreams for a big salary and a fancy job title. Wouldn't it be a shame if all you had to show for your life were a $300,000 home, a hot tub, 42-inch TV and a Jeep Grand Cherokee?

In the long run, do you really think your happiness and satisfaction with life boils down to what you own?

Myth #7: Retirement Planning is Complicated

If the first six myths haven't put the fear into you yet, this myth is enough to lead you astray. Most of us have been led to believe that retirement planning is a daunting and complicated task. The average person doesn't have the knowledge or training to understand it.

No wonder most people let the experts take care of it. After all, do you really want to spend what little free time you have poring over complex graphs, charts and numbers on mutual funds, equities, RRIFs, LIFs, annuities, and the dizzying array of other financial issues aimed at the retirement market?

It is enough to make your eyes glaze over. Or drive you to caffeine, nicotine or the bottle out of worry and anxiety about the future. Why not sit back and let someone else look after everything? All you have to do is write the cheque or authorize an automatic debit on your savings account. Your financial advisor will take care of the rest.

Think about it for a minute. Do you really believe that a stranger cares as much about your money as you do? A surprising number of people hand over their retirement portfolio to an advisor—and give up control of their future without a second thought.

Come on. You don't really think your advisor stays up at night worrying about your portfolio, do you? Most people in the field will put the best spin on things because they want to make a sale.

Who do you think has your best interests at heart? The face you see in the mirror every day, or a commission-based salesperson?

Personally, we would bet on the face in the mirror. If you want to retire early, it is essential that you take an active role in your own retirement planning.

Planning for your retirement is a lot simpler than you think. All it takes is some basic research. You don't need anything more sophisticated than a pencil and paper, and a basic calculator, to do some simple number crunching.

The following three questions need to be answered:

> How much money will I realistically need to retire on?
> How much will I get from pensions and other sources?
> How much savings will I need to bridge the gap between my expenses and pension benefits?

Interestingly, most retirement advice ignores these basic questions. Why waste your time looking at household budgeting, they say, when you should be focusing on improving your financial situation instead. Somehow this strikes us as the hard way to do things.

4:

You Need a Lot Less Than You Think

Imagine sorting through your mail one day and, to your astonishment, finding an embossed invitation from Buckingham Palace nestled among the usual pile of flyers, junk mail and bills. The Queen has personally requested your presence for tea and scones. Hopefully, you get to hear some juicy gossip on the latest palace scandals.

Sorry, we hate to dash your hopes. But the reality of this happening is about the same probability as the average person saving a million dollars. In fact, you might have a better chance of actually getting that invitation.

It is no surprise that many people shelve their early retirement dreams and end up working years longer than they need to. Or they are scared out of their wits into saving far more than they really have to.

Now a good kick in the pants, for some, to start saving may not be such a bad thing. Just don't start blindly salting too much money away without knowing what you really require. There is no point in sacrificing your youth, and your health, for the sake of a large retirement nest egg.

Chances are you don't need one anyway. Have you ever considered that all that money won't matter if your family and friends are strangers? In view of all the long hours you're putting in, are you really surprised? Or your health is shot. In that case, you won't live long enough to spend your hard-earned cash, anyway.

So How Much do You Need?

You're now ready to find out. The two worksheets in this chapter will guide you through the process.

Worksheet 1 helps you identify and calculate the costs you have right now, but won't have once you retire.

Worksheet 2 adds in health, prescription, optical and dental costs. These may be currently covered under your employee benefits plan. Don't forget that once you're retired, you'll have to cover these costs yourself. *Worksheet 2* also adds in income tax, and a contingency fund to cover unexpected expenses. The figure you are left with is how much retirement income you will need. There's no reason to worry. The figure you calculate will still provide you with the same comfortable lifestyle you have right now.

Before you get started, we should point something out. Don't be concerned about accounting for everything you have spent over the last year. Unless you have been tracking every cent, this would be impossible to know anyway. For now, the figures you come up with in *Worksheets 1* and *2* will give you a preliminary estimate of how much money you will need in retirement.

Once you have read Part Two of this book, and start recording your actual spending, you can go back and revise your numbers. You will then have a more accurate estimate of your retirement costs, and the resulting savings you will need.

Discovering Costs You Won't Have

Okay. Let's get started. You are ready to add up all those expenses you have now, but won't have once you are retired.

Housing
One of the biggest expenses for most people is the cost of housing. Your goal should be to have your house paid off by the time you retire. The trick to early retirement is to

get your fixed living costs as low as possible. This is hard to do if you are making hefty house payments.

Record the amount of your monthly mortgage payment on *Worksheet 1*.

Going to Work

It's ironic, isn't it, how it costs money to earn money? The costs of going to work can add up fast. To find out what your work-related expenses are, add up:

> Deductions that are regularly taken off of your paycheque like income tax, employer pension plan contributions, CPP/EI deductions, and union or professional dues.
> Costs related to your job such as transportation costs, parking fees, work clothes, lunches, coffee and snacks, and work-related social events.
> Childcare fees, if you have young children.

Granted, your income will be smaller once you're no longer working. But look on the bright side. You will also be paying less income tax, and will no longer have pension contributions or deductions for employment insurance, and professional and union dues. There's no need to budget for childcare fees anymore either.

Don't forget, as well, the money you will save on gas, maintenance, parking and insurance. Now that you're not driving your car to work, your car will last years longer. If you take a bus to work, you'll save on bus tickets or a bus pass, and can look forward to your discounted senior's pass one day. Who said getting older was so bad?

Work-related clothing costs will also go down considerably. There will be no need to dress up. After all, who needs fancy clothes when you're gardening, out for a bike ride, volunteering, or even sailing off to Samoa? Even if you've been diligently brown bagging it and saving your money, just the cost of a coffee a day and the occasional lunch out can add up fast.

Estimate what your work-related costs are and record these on *Worksheet 1*.

Raising Children

If you have children, and they are still living at home, you will know that raising children isn't cheap. Once you retire, these day-to-day expenses are over. You hope. Of course your kids may decide the family nest they couldn't wait to leave after high school wasn't so bad after all, and they move back in.

Obviously, if your children have left home already, or you don't have any children, you can ignore this expense.

To help you estimate what you are currently spending on raising your children each year, add up what you spend on:

> ➢ Fees for sports, music lessons, camps and any other extracurricular activities your children have been involved in over the past year, along with equipment costs. These are probably the easiest to

remember. Don't forget to divide this number by twelve to get a monthly figure.

➤ School-related expenses such as fees, supplies and field trips.

➤ Dental bills. Even if you are lucky enough to have a dental plan through your work, your portion of costly procedures like braces, crowns, root canals or wisdom teeth removal can add up pretty fast. Again, divide the total cost by twelve to get an average monthly cost.

➤ Clothes, haircuts and other personal items.

➤ Groceries. Don't forget items like school lunches and after-school snacks that you would not normally buy just for the two of you. Take an educated guess at how much extra you are spending on food.

➤ Any other expenses.

With two teenage boys living at home, one of our biggest monthly expenses is our grocery bill. Our food costs, especially our snack food category, should drop considerably once they move out. If it doesn't, and you realize that you're the one who's been wolfing down the junk food all these years, it's time to start paying attention to your health—and your waistline. You'll save money and live longer too. You do want to enjoy your retirement, don't you?

Record your estimated monthly child-raising costs on *Worksheet 1*. You'll have to take an educated guess at some of these costs. Later, when you start tracking your spending, you can come back and revise your estimates. Go with your ballpark figure for now.

Credit Card/Other Debt Payments

Realistically, you shouldn't think about early retirement until you are debt-free. If you are making any of the following payments, make it a priority to get your financial house in order before you retire, and eliminate things like:

> - Line of credit payments.
> - Credit card payments.
> - Car payments.
> - Other debt payments.

You won't have any money left over to enjoy yourself if you are stuck paying off bills when you retire. There is no point in retiring early in that case. You'll be too stressed out. You are better off working until your debts are paid off.

Calculate the monthly costs for any loans that you are currently paying off.

Record these figures on *Worksheet 1*.

Savings

Once you are retired, you won't need to put aside money for the following any more:

> ➢ Registered Retirement Savings Plans (RRSPs), or money that you regularly put away each month into bank accounts, or things like bonds, Guaranteed Investment Certificates (GICs), or mutual funds.
> ➢ Savings for your children's education, such as Registered Education Savings Plans (RESPs).

Record how much you are saving each month on *Worksheet 1*.

Worksheet 1: Retirement Expenses You Won't Have

Housing
    Mortgage Payments $_____

Costs of Working
    All Deductions off Your Paycheque $_____
    Work Clothes $_____
    Lunches, Coffee, Social Fund, Gifts $_____
    Commuting Costs $_____
    Childcare Fees $_____

Costs of Raising Children
    Fees and Equipment Costs of Extra-
    curricular Activities (eg. sports, music) $_____
    School Fees, Supplies, Field Trips $_____
    Dental and Other Related Health Costs $_____
    Clothes, Haircuts, Other Personal Items $_____
    Groceries (including snack food, school $_____
    lunches)

Debts
    Line of Credit Payments $_____
    Paying off Credit Card Bills $_____
    Car Payments $_____
    Other $_____

Savings
    Retirement Savings $_____
    Savings for Your Children's Education $_____

Costs You Won't Have Monthly Total   (A) $_____

How Much Retirement Income Do You Need?

Hold on. Before you get too excited about how much cheaper retirement will be, there are some extra costs that you need to take into account. These expenses will be recorded in *Worksheet 2*.

Health-Related Costs

Once you leave your job you lose some of those health-related benefits you may have enjoyed. The exception, of course, is if you are self-employed, and have already been covering these costs yourself. People living in British Columbia, for example, will now have to pay all of their health care premiums, as will those living in Alberta until they are sixty-five.

If you retire early, you'll also have to cover your own dental costs, prescription drugs and optical costs—at least until you become eligible for any senior's discounts and benefits that are available in your province.

The easy part is accounting for your health-related expenses right now. Add up the costs of healthcare premiums, if you now have to pay these. Think back to what you have spent over the past year on dentists, prescriptions, new glasses, and any medical treatments.

Do you have to take drugs for a chronic health condition? Do you suffer from back problems and frequently see a chiropractor or massage therapist for relief? Pull your receipts out, if you have saved them, and add them up. If not, take an educated guess at your current costs.

The hard part is figuring out your future medical costs. If you are in good health now, chances are you may not need a lot extra. But if your health is poor, and you anticipate having a lot of health problems in your old age, be sure to account for these costs in your budget.

You will have to take your best guess at these expenses. In order to keep costs manageable, you might want to sign up for extra health and prescription coverage, such as Blue Cross.

It is difficult to predict what the future holds. Your best bet is to take preventive action. Eat right, exercise and make it a priority to take care of your health right now. This can help you avoid high medical bills when you are retired, and ensure you have a healthy and active retirement.

Record your projected health care costs including health care premiums, and those costs currently covered by your employer, in *Worksheet 2*.

Contingency Fund

For your own peace of mind, it is a good idea to add a monthly contingency fund into your budget to pay for unexpected expenses. These always seem to come up when you least expect them.

The furnace breaks down, your car develops a major mechanical problem, or you want to enroll in that advanced weaving course in Mexico that you've always dreamed about. You name it. There's always something to spend money on. We use ten percent but the amount is really up to you. It all depends on the kind of lifestyle you expect to have in retirement.

While we can control our consumer spending one of the biggest unknowns is the cost of energy. In the last couple of years we have seen these costs skyrocket. There is nothing more frustrating than watching heating and electrical costs soar even as you adjust your thermostat down and try to use less electricity.

Property taxes are another unknown, although one thing is guaranteed. They will go up. This is especially true if the value of your house has been increasing lately. Don't feel too bad. The silver lining is that the value of your investment is appreciating in value. You can also expect your condo fees to increase, if you live in a condominium. After all, have they ever gone down?

Another unknown is car insurance. Those of us unlucky to live in a province without public automobile insurance have seen a large increase in premiums in the last few years.

Record the amount of your contingency fund in *Worksheet 2*. Our contingency fund, as we said earlier, is ten percent of our gross annual retirement income. Choose an amount you feel comfortable with.

Income Tax

You'll notice *Worksheet 2* adds in an estimate of the income tax payable on your retirement income. Come on, no long faces here. Did you really think Revenue Canada would reward you for your long years of service as a taxpayer, and give you a break now that you are retired?

Cheer up. If you plan it right, you should be able to minimize your tax bill. Keep in mind that you pay a low rate of tax on the first portion of your taxable income, and higher rates the more you earn.

Provincial tax rates and credits vary considerably. The simplest way to figure out how much income tax you will need to pay is to pull out last year's income tax statement. Look up how much income tax you will owe, based on the retirement income that you calculated you would need. Divide this figure by twelve to get a monthly estimate of your tax bill.

Keep in mind this is a rough estimate for now. In Chapter Eight you will look at some strategies for minimizing your tax bill.

Worksheet 2: How Much Money Do You Need?

Gross Monthly Income While
Working

    You   + _____

    Your Partner   + _____

    Total Household Income   = _____   ▶ _____

Subtract Costs You Won't Have
(Total "A" from Worksheet 1)   - _____

                                           = _____

Add Health-Related Expenses   + _____

                               (B)   = _____

Add Contingency Fund
(eg. 10% of 'B')   + _____

Total Monthly Pre-Tax
Retirement Income Needed   = _____

Annual Pre-Tax Retirement
Income Needed   x 12   = _____

Add Annual Income Tax Payable   + _____

Gross Annual Retirement Income
Needed   = _____

Gross Monthly Retirement
Income Needed   ÷ 12   = _____

How Far From Seventy Percent Are You?

Just out of curiosity, what percentage of your gross working income do you need to live on once you are retired? To find out:

> ➢ Multiply your projected annual retirement income from *Worksheet 2* by one hundred.
> ➢ Divide this figure by your gross annual household income, or the money that you are currently earning while you are working.

Is this anywhere near the seventy percent the experts say you need? If it is under, congratulations! You've got the idea. However, if it is more, you need to seriously look at trimming your costs. You know by now that it is easier to reduce your costs than to earn more money, or to save more.

With a little imagination and creativity, you can easily pare down your retirement costs even further.

Now that you've paid off the mortgage, you may want to reduce your housing costs even more. Why not move into a smaller house or into a condominium?

Or, what about a cheaper area? After all, you don't need to worry about commuting anymore. This means you can be a lot more flexible where you live, and the bonus is that you will save on property taxes, maintenance and utilities.

You could pocket the difference to finance a year or more of your early retirement. The big advantage, of course, is that you have to save that much less.

You could also sell off one car. Better yet, get rid of your cars altogether if you live in an area with decent transit service. Sure, this is a tough psychological hurdle for most people. After all, we've become addicted to the convenience cars provide.

Don't forget this convenience comes at a cost. You have to consider if it's worth it, especially when you factor in skyrocketing insurance premiums and the rising cost of gas—not to mention all those repair and maintenance bills.

The fact is it's cheaper to take taxis, rent a car when you need one, take public transit, or walk. Think of your sacrifice this way. Not only are you taking better care of your health, but you're also doing your own small part to make our planet more sustainable. Now that should make you feel good, shouldn't it?

What else can you come up with?

Now This is More Like It

Not surprisingly, if you ignore the seventy percent rule of thumb retirement planners routinely use, you need to save a lot less money. A cookie-cutter approach doesn't take into account your lifestyle and personal situation. Consider the following example.

Gillian is divorced and has no children. She earns $52,000 a year, which works out to just over $4,300 a month. If she applied the seventy percent figure she is told she needs to retire on, Gillian would require a retirement income of $36,400, or about three thousand dollars a month.

Fortunately, she worked through the numbers herself. To her surprise, she found she could live quite comfortably on $24,000 (in today's dollars). This is equivalent to forty-six percent of her working income, or two thousand dollars a month.

If this figure seems small, don't forget it is all disposable income. Gillian's house is paid for and she is debt-free.

There is an obvious advantage to setting your own rule of thumb. If Gillian had listened to the experts, she would need to save an extra thousand dollars a month to live on. This works out to twelve thousand dollars more a year. If she had to set up a pool of capital to generate that extra income, she would need to save an additional $240,000, assuming five percent returns.

How many extra years of working would it take you to save this much?

5:

Where Will It Come From?

Well done! You've crunched the numbers and done the math. Now you know how much money you need to live on. The next step is to figure out where you are going to get it.

This is a simple question to answer when you are working. Your income comes primarily from one source—your job. In retirement, your income may come from a combination of three sources: government pension programs, work pensions, and personal savings.

If you were to embrace the seven retirement myths we talked about earlier, your retirement financial planning would be driven by the following logic:

> ➢ Don't count on government pension programs when you are ready to retire. Even in the unlikely event they are still around when you need them, the benefits won't amount to much. Or else they will only be available to poor folks on the bread line.
> ➢ Your work pension won't be nearly enough to meet all of your retirement needs.
> ➢ Your best bet is to look to your own personal savings and assets.

The net result of following this line of reasoning is to play down, or even dismiss altogether, the value of your work and government pensions. In actual fact, government pension programs and work pension benefits—assuming you are one of the lucky ones to get one—will make up a substantial part of most people's retirement income.

To plan your retirement you need to find out exactly how much they are worth.

What to Expect from Government Pensions

The federal government has two main retirement income programs: Old Age Security and the Canada Pension Plan. The purpose of these plans is to ensure retirees have a modest, but significant, income base to work from. Retirees are expected to top up these two levels of funding by an employer pension and/or their own personal savings.

Old Age Security

OAS is a universal program that everyone is entitled to, whether you have worked outside the home or not. To get the full pension you must be sixty-five, a Canadian citizen or legal resident, and have lived in Canada for forty years after your eighteenth birthday.

You still qualify for benefits even if you have only lived in Canada for ten years after your 18th birthday. But they will be reduced.

The maximum OAS income, at the time of writing, is almost $472 per month. This works out to over $5,600 a year for a single person. A couple will get well over eleven thousand dollars a year. The rates go up with inflation and are reviewed and adjusted in January, April, July and October every year.

An annual OAS benefit of $5,600 may not seem like a big deal. To put it into perspective, think about how much you would have to save to get an equivalent amount. At a modest four percent interest rate, you would need a

$140,000 pool of capital to get a return of $5,600 every year. Suddenly OAS benefits look a lot more attractive, don't they?

Don't Wait for a Birthday Card and Cheque

We should warn you, though. Don't sit back and wait for the government to automatically send you birthday greetings and money once you turn sixty-five. You have to apply for this benefit if you want to take advantage of it.

Be sure you leave enough time to get the paperwork done. That's why it is a good idea to send in your application at least six months before you turn sixty-five.

The process itself is simple. If you have a computer at home, all you have to do is download an application form from the federal Department of Social Development's website (www.dsd-mds.gc.ca). Or, you could call and request that an application be mailed to you.

Clawbacks

Your basic OAS pension is considered taxable income. If you earn too much money you can expect to have some, or even all, of your OAS benefits clawed back. At the time of writing, the threshold income was $59,790. Note that this is net individual income. For every dollar of income above this amount you lose fifteen cents.

To explain how this works, let's say you earned $65,000 in net taxable income. You would be above the clawback threshold by $5,210. This means you would lose $781 in OAS income a year, or sixty-five dollars a month. All of your OAS benefits will be clawed back if you are pulling in about $97,000 in net income.

Obviously, repaying benefits will not be a big issue for most people. Currently, only five percent of seniors receive reduced OAS pensions, and two percent lose the entire amount.

Guaranteed Income Supplement

If you don't have much money other than OAS benefits, you can also apply for the Guaranteed Income Supplement (GIS) and the Allowance.

The GIS is extra money on top of the OAS payment, and is intended for low-income seniors. In order to qualify for GIS money, you must be receiving OAS payments and meet their income requirements. The cut-off income for the GIS varies, depending on your situation.

If your spouse is also a pensioner, GIS benefits stop being paid when your combined income is $17,568 or more. If your spouse is a non-pensioner, you will not receive benefits if your combined income is over $32,592. If you are single, you are not eligible for benefits if you make more than $13,464. At the time of writing, the maximum monthly GIS benefit varied from $560 for a single person to $365 if you are the spouse of a pensioner.

Keep in mind that you don't have to count any of your OAS benefits as income when you apply for GIS benefits. You do have to report all other sources of income, though. This includes CPP benefits, workplace pension plans,

RRSPs, interest on any savings, capital gains or dividends, and income from any rental properties.

The Allowance

This is another OAS program for low-income seniors. It provides a monthly benefit to seniors between the ages of sixty and sixty-four who are spouses, or common-law partners, of OAS pensioners. The purpose of the program is to bridge the gap until both partners can collect OAS benefits.

At the time of writing, the average Allowance paid out was about $315 per month. It can go as high as $837 a month. The amount you get depends on how low your income is. The Allowance stops being paid when the combined income of you and your partner is just over $25,000 a year.

GIS and Allowance benefits are adjusted for inflation every three months. Although OAS benefits are considered taxable income, and must be declared on your income tax return each year, the GIS and the Allowance are not taxable. Even so, you still have to report them on your tax return.

You Need to Apply

We should caution you. Don't sit back and wait to be showered with GIS and Allowance money. You have to apply for the benefits if you want to get them.

We recently read that more than 300,000 seniors who are eligible for the GIS supplement are not collecting any benefits. It has been estimated that this is saving the federal government $500 million a year. Obviously the federal government has no big incentive to encourage you to apply. That leaves it up to you. Find out what you are eligible for. Can you think of a good reason to pass up money you are entitled to?

Also keep in mind that you have to renew your application every year if you want to keep receiving GIS and Allowance benefits. The rationale for this is pretty straightforward. The government wants to ensure your circumstances have not changed, and that you still qualify for this extra money.

Most seniors automatically renew their benefits by filing their income tax return by April 30th. If you don't file a tax return, you can ask that a renewal application form be mailed to you.

Canada Pension Plan

Although the CPP is commonly referred to as a government pension plan, this is misleading. It is really a government-sponsored plan, not a government pension.

This money is yours. Contrary to what some people might think, it is not a handout. Think of it as deferred savings that you and your employer have been putting aside for years for your retirement.

You and your employer fully fund the plan through your fifty/fifty contribution. The federal government doesn't chip in a cent. All they do is keep the money in safekeeping for you, and manage it through an arm's length Board on your behalf. Naturally, at some point, you want your money back, right?

You should keep in mind that the rules governing CPP monies are different from Old Age Security. CPP is not a universal program. You only get your money back if you have contributed to the plan. The amount you get depends on how long you work and how much money you earn. This affects how much you pay into it and ultimately collect.

You are not eligible to collect CPP benefits if you have never worked outside the home. This means homemakers don't get any benefits, although there have been several requests over the years to have this reviewed.

The good news is that you can apply to have some low earnings periods removed from the calculation. This includes the years you stayed home to raise your children up to the age of seven, or fifteen percent of your lowest earning years. The advantage of not counting these low earnings periods is that they won't reduce your future benefits.

Currently, the average CPP retirement benefit at sixty-five is $446 a month. The maximum benefit is $814 a month which works out to just shy of ten thousand dollars a year. The pension is designed to replace about twenty-five percent of the average wage. Payments are increased every January to keep up with inflation.

Once you start collecting your CPP pension, you can work as much as you want without affecting your pension payment, but you are not allowed to contribute to it anymore.

Deciding When to Collect

Like other federal pension benefits, you have to apply to receive Canada Pension Plan payments. The CPP has an added advantage. You can decide when you would like to start collecting your benefits. You can start as early as the age of sixty, or wait until you are seventy.

It stands to reason your pension is smaller if you take it earlier, and larger if you take it later. The amount is decreased by 0.5% for each month that you start your pension before your sixty-fifth birthday and increased by 0.5% for each month after your sixty-fifth birthday. This adjustment is permanent. You can't start collecting and then change your mind.

Avoid the mistake a lot of people make. Don't put off collecting your benefits. Start as soon as you can. At first glance, it might make sense to wait until you are sixty-five and collect your full benefits, or even hold off until you are seventy and collect 130% of your benefits. However, there are three convincing reasons to take the cash as soon as you can.

First of all, do you know when you are going to die? The rationale for waiting would make more sense if you knew you were going to live to a ripe old age. But the reality is, unless you have a crystal ball, no one knows with certainty. That's why you shouldn't wait to collect money you are entitled to. Incidentally, this is generally a good rule of thumb to follow in any case.

For example, let's say that you waited until you were sixty-five. Three months later you are out on the golf course and suffer a massive heart attack. Sure, you got three months of full benefits—not that this is any compensation to your widow. However, if you had started taking the cash when you were sixty, you would have had five years and three months of benefits. Even at thirty percent less, you are still much further ahead financially. That's because every month you wait, you have to live longer to collect it back.

Second, another good reason for putting the money in your pocket now, rather than later, is that you can spend it while you are young, healthy and more active. At this stage of your life, you are still what gerontologists refer to as "go-go's". As you get older, you become a "slow-go", and then finally a "no-go". It makes sense to take the cash while you're still a "go-go".

Sure. We've all read of seniors skydiving well into their eighties. Despite our hope to remain active far into our old age, realistically speaking, adventurous oldtimers like these are definitely the exception. Most people slow down, and often it's not by choice, but as a result of poor health. Let's face it. It is pretty hard to remain on the go when you're suffering from painful arthritis and it hurts to move, or your eyesight is failing. It only makes sense to take the money now—while you can still enjoy it.

Third, you want to keep your tax bill as low as possible. An easy way to do this is to split your income with your partner. If one person has been a higher wage earner, and stands to get a larger CPP benefit, they are allowed to assign half their CPP income to their partner. The catch is both you and your partner have to be at least sixty. If you take your CPP benefits early, you get a tax advantage years sooner than if you had waited to sixty-five to collect. We'll talk more about reducing your tax bill later in Chapter Eight.

Convinced, yet? We hope so.

Getting an Updated Statement of Contributions

Did you know that you are allowed to request a Statement of Contributions once every year? This will tell you how much money you can expect to get from the Canada Pension Plan once you retire. We would suggest that you request the statement in July, or three months after you file your tax return in order to get the most up-to-date information.

It is easy to apply online. Log on to the federal Department of Social Development's website at www.dsd-mds.gc.ca. Select whether you would like the text in English or French, click on "Seniors" and then "Statement of Contributions". It takes less than a minute to fill out the form online.

All you need to have on hand is your social insurance number, home postal code and daytime phone number. Or, you can call the federal Department of Social

Development free of charge at 1-877-454-4051 to request an estimate.

Obviously, you want to get a pension estimate well before you retire. We'd suggest you get one five years before you actually quit your job. This will give you a good idea of how much money you can expect to collect. This will help with your retirement planning. Don't be afraid to ask for updated estimates the closer that you get to retirement. These will be more accurate than your earlier estimates.

Cashing in For Life With Government Benefits

Government pension cheques make up a big portion of most people's retirement income. We don't want to lecture or dwell on this point, but we can't stress enough that you need to find out how much you can expect to get. Once you have the information, you can then determine how much you need to save. More importantly, you'll know how much longer you need to keep working. That's a pretty good incentive to become informed, isn't it?

As we've mentioned before, an excellent resource is the federal Department of Social Development's website (www.dsd-mds.gc.ca). The different types of federal government pensions available are explained, along with criteria for qualifying, and average monthly benefits for each program. There's also a calculator that provides you with a personalized estimate of the benefits you are entitled to, based on your income. Benefit amounts are up-to-date. They are changed regularly to reflect adjustments to the cost of living.

The big advantage of online access is convenience. You can download the necessary application forms and apply for your benefits right from the comfort of your own home. There's absolutely no need to change out of your housecoat and bedroom slippers, dress up and drive downtown.

If you don't have a computer at home, just head down to your nearest public library. It's been our experience that librarians are generally happy to lend a hand. They can help if you have any questions about accessing information.

Work Pensions

Did you know that less than half of working Canadians, or just under forty percent, has a work pension plan? The good news is that those who do stand to get a significant pension income. This is especially true if they work for a large corporation, or in the public service.

The money you get from a work pension is over and above what federal government pension programs pay out. Typically, the amount depends on your years of service and how much you earned while you worked.

Make Sure You Have a Plan

At the risk of sounding blunt, what do you know about your work pension plan? There's a reason for asking. A retirement awareness study conducted by Statistics Canada in 2001 had some astonishing results. They found that an estimated 390,000 full time permanent employees in the private sector, or four per cent of the total, thought they had a retirement plan. It turns out they didn't. Can you imagine their surprise when they retire?

Sure, we know this sounds bizarre. But confirm with your employer that you do in fact have a pension plan. Ask for a copy of their pension booklet. Find out how the plan works and how much you are eligible for.

You should be able to obtain a copy of a statement of your benefits. This will provide information such as your years of credited service, you and your employer's contributions over the past year, the pension benefit you earned over the year, and your expected date of retirement. Don't forget to ask what the payment options are, and their effect on how much money you will receive.

Many larger employers, such as government, have websites with a pension calculator. The calculator is a great tool. It can provide you with a reasonably accurate estimate of how much money you can expect to get. Try a number of scenarios out by inputting different retirement ages.

Who knows? You might get a pleasant surprise and find out you can afford to retire years sooner than you think.

What Are You Hanging On For?

It continues to amaze us how many people insist on working until they qualify for a full pension. It doesn't seem to matter if they are in poor health or detest their job. They are determined to hang in there, no matter what personal sacrifices they have to make, so they can collect every cent they are eligible for.

We suppose you can't really blame them. It just goes to show how the wealth management industry has terrified future retirees. They are scared they won't have enough money in their old age. That's too bad. If people took the time to do the math they would realize they don't need nearly as much as they think they do.

More importantly, have you ever considered the money won't do you any good if you don't live long enough to enjoy it?

Work Pension Options

If you have changed jobs frequently throughout your career, you have a few choices about what you can do with your accumulated company pension benefits. If you have worked at a job less than five years, and your pension isn't vested or locked-in, you can take a cash refund. Don't go and live it up, though. Save the money for something important, like your early retirement.

If your pension is vested, or locked-in, you have two options. You can either keep your accumulated pension

our former employer's pension plan fund,
your money out.

n't get too excited. This doesn't mean you
convert this windfall into cash, and spend it on your
dream vacation, or that car you have always wanted.
Neither the federal or provincial governments allow
this—for good reason. They want to make sure your
locked-in funds are used to provide pension income for
you once you retire.

If you decide to take your money out, you must
convert your accumulated pension money into a locked-in
RRSP or Locked-In Retirement Account (LIRA) until you
are ready to retire. Don't get confused by the different
names. What they are called depends on the province
where you live. These locked-in accounts are similar to an
RRSP in that you have the same flexibility in deciding
how to invest your money.

RRSPs and Locked-In RRSPs

There are two key differences between a regular RRSP
and a locked-in RRSP, or LIRA.

First of all, you can't withdraw your funds from a
locked-in RRSP or LIRA until you reach a certain age.
This varies, depending on provincial legislation and the
normal retirement age for your pension plan.

Second, you have less flexibility in how you withdraw
your locked-in funds once you reach this age. You can
either purchase a life annuity, or transfer your money to a

Life Income Fund (LIF), or Life Retirement Income Fund (LRIF).

The important thing to keep in mind is to make sure you fully understand the restrictions around various options. Inform yourself before you make any decisions about your pension savings so that you're well aware of the consequences that may result.

If you have a work pension plan a lot of the heavy financial lifting has been done for you. Go out and celebrate. You may not need to save a cent of your own money. Of course if you plan on joining the cocktail circuit and travelling in a stretch limo once you retire, that's a different matter. Somehow we don't think that is the kind of retirement most people have in mind.

Personal Savings

Most people will need a modest nest egg. How much depends on a number of factors. This includes your expected lifestyle, how creative you are at keeping your costs down, and how young you are when you retire.

Obviously, it stands to reason you'll need more of your own personal savings if you retire before you are eligible to collect any pension money. Keep in mind that the earliest you can collect Canada Pension Plan benefits is sixty. You won't qualify for Old Age Security until the age of sixty-five. Many workplace pensions don't start before the age of fifty-five.

Your personal savings fall into three types: government regulated plans such as Registered Retirement Savings Plans (RRSPs), other savings and assets.

Advantages of RRSPs

Most of us have opened an RRSP at one time or another. The federal government introduced RRSPs to encourage people to save for their retirement. Putting money in an RRSP has two advantages. First of all, you can claim a tax deduction for that contribution.

Second, you can keep the income generated from investments inside your RRSP tax deferred until you withdraw it from the plan. This tax deferral feature of the RRSP allows you to accumulate larger savings for your retirement than if you invested outside the RRSP. That's because you're not paying any taxes on your interest income, at least for now anyway. Keep in mind that you can contribute to an RRSP until the end of the year in which you turn sixty-nine.

When to Avoid RRSPs

Before we go any further, we should point out that RRSPs are not a good idea for everyone. Avoid them, for example, if you think you will have a modest income when you retire. In that case, they would be a definite disadvantage. That's because every dollar you add to your income will reduce, or even disqualify you from receiving, all of the federal pension benefits you might otherwise get, such as GIS monies.

You would be better off investing your money outside an RRSP. You can use your unsheltered money to "top up" your retirement income, and it won't have any impact on your GIS entitlement. It also won't affect your tax bill. This money is not counted as income. That's because you have already declared this money as income and paid tax on it when you earned it.

Having said that, RRSPs are still a good savings tool for most people. Just don't forget that there is a day of reckoning. The same government that gave you the initial tax deduction for your contributions will want to be paid back when you cash in your RRSPs.

When you eventually withdraw your savings from the plan, you have to count this as taxable income in the year that you receive the money. Your financial institution will withhold the following amounts:

Income Tax Withheld When RRSPs are Cashed In

Withdrawal Amount	Withholding Tax	Quebec
0 to $5,000	10%	25%
$5,001 - $15,000	20%	33%
$15,000 and up	30%	38%

Any money remaining in your RRSPs on December 31 of the year when you turn sixty-nine must be withdrawn in a lump sum, converted into a Registered Retirement Income Fund (RRIF), or used to purchase an annuity. You can also do any combination of these three alternatives.

Choosing the lump sum option can be costly and we wouldn't recommend it. You will have to declare this money as income for that tax year. This means you could be stuck paying a hefty tax bill. There's no point in saving your money if you can't keep it, is there?

Registered Retirement Income Fund (RRIF)

A Registered Retirement Income Fund (RRIF) is one way of avoiding having to cash out your RRSPs. Your principal and accumulated earnings remain tax-sheltered. You can continue to hold the same assets as you do in your RRSP—including guaranteed investment certificates, savings accounts, term deposits, bonds and mutual funds—and have as many RRIFs as you want.

However, unlike an RRSP, you can no longer make tax-deductible contributions. As well, there is a minimum amount you have to take out each year. It is calculated as a percentage of your total assets in the RRIF. The rate goes up the older you get. For example, when you turn seventy, current rules state you have to withdraw five percent of your RRIF assets. It's just shy of ten percent when you are eighty-four.

You have the flexibility to purchase an annuity with all or part of your savings in the RRIF. The funds in a RRIF become part of your estate when you die.

Annuities

An annuity is basically a contract between you and a life insurance company. In return for your money, you receive a guaranteed income for a defined time period.

The interest rates in effect at the time of purchase are a factor in how much you get. The disadvantage, of course, is that you could be locked into an annuity based on a low interest rate. Not surprisingly, annuities are popular during periods when interest rates are high.

Annuities are based on mortality tables and your life expectancy, or the number of years between your current age and your anticipated age at death. This helps to determine how long payments will be made to you.

Everything else being equal, the older you are when you purchase an annuity, the higher the payment. Women receive lower payments than men of the same age. That's because they can expect to live longer and collect more money.

Buying an annuity is much like buying a car. There are a lot of options you can choose from. Most are variations of the two basic annuity types: life and fixed term. You get less money once you start adding guarantee options, keeping in mind that the trade-off is security. For example, most people are willing to receive lower payments to ensure that their partner continues getting benefits when they die.

Choose the option that best meets your needs. Just be sure that you understand the implications, as your choice will affect how much money you receive.

Other Savings

Other savings include bank accounts, term deposits, guaranteed investment certificates, stocks, mutual funds, stock dividends, Canada Savings Bonds, real estate and equity in a business. These can provide you with additional income in your retirement.

If you are holding these investments outside an RRSP or LIRA, they are easier to access. There are also no age restrictions for when they can be cashed in. Even so, they still may have some of their own limitations for cashing in.

For example, a fixed term non-redeemable GIC has to be held until maturity. You should be aware of what restrictions there are. It's also a good idea to be aware of the income tax implications of your investments, as they can vary depending on the type of investment.

Assets

Assets are things that you own that you could sell to supplement your retirement income. This includes things like your house, vehicle, antique furniture and recreational property.

Keep in mind that the value of your assets is based on what others are willing to pay for them, not on what you think they are worth. For that matter, it may not even be based on what they have been appraised at.

Consider this reality if you are planning to sell off a prized family heirloom to help finance your retirement. After all, you don't want to be disappointed with what it brings in, especially if you were hoping for a substantial windfall.

Aging Has its Financial Rewards

Yes, Virginia, there really is a Santa Claus. Seniors, at any rate, have good reason to believe in him. The older you get, the more money you are showered with. Who said getting old was so bad?

Timing For Cashing In

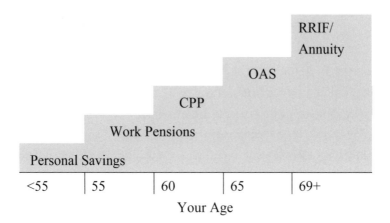

Notice how your income grows, as you get older? This means you'll have to plan your retirement in phases to account for these differences in cash flow.

Keep in mind that you will be relying heavily on your personal savings to pay the bills if you retire before age fifty-five. After that, work pension benefits, assuming you have a company pension plan, often kick in. You are eligible for early CPP benefits at age sixty. Together, these two benefits will help carry a lot of the financial burden.

By the time you celebrate your sixty-fifth birthday, and begin receiving OAS benefits, you may not need any personal savings at all. At any rate, the amount will be far less than when you first retired.

When you are sixty-nine you will have to convert any registered retirement savings you are holding into a RRIF or an annuity, and start withdrawing this money, further adding to your retirement income.

Don't Save More Than You Need

You may actually find yourself having more money than you can spend, as you get older. Hold on a minute. This is no reason to pop open the champagne. Too much money just shows poor planning on your part. It means you didn't consider all of your income sources. The consequence, of course, is that you scrimped and sacrificed more than you needed to, and you probably worked longer than you had to.

It doesn't make a lot of sense to throw away your prime years working long, exhausting hours so that you can save a pile of cash for your old age. It comes at a big personal cost. You're trading off your family and your friends for your job. Yet, crazy as it seems, saving the big pile of cash is conventional retirement advice.

Too Much Money Creates a Lot of Headaches

Ironically, your sacrifice may be for nothing anyway. What do you plan on spending all your money on? Don't forget you are getting older and less active. As people age, most are content to putter around the yard. They have also bought most of the consumer items they need.

The standard advice is to reinvest your extra cash. But just how long do you expect to live anyway? Who do you plan on leaving all your money to?

At the risk of belabouring the point, don't forget, as well, that your income taxes will go up once you starting withdrawing your investments. Even if you haven't touched any of your RRSP assets to this point, there is a day of reckoning when you turn sixty-nine. RRSP rules require that you start cashing them in.

You don't get any tax breaks when the money is withdrawn as it is taxed in the same way as employment income.

Finally, have you ever considered that you may be worth more dead than alive? Disconcerting, isn't it?

There is a better solution. If you find yourself with more money than you can spend why not just give out the cash to your heirs in person? Think of how nice it will feel to get a heartfelt thank-you note from your grateful relatives.

6:

Tips on Crunching the Numbers

It's time to do some serious number crunching now, and figure out your own situation. You should have a pretty good idea of how much money you need, and where you will get it from. All you have left to do is add up your income sources, and figure out how much you need to save. It's that easy.

Before we get started, let's look at a couple of examples first.

Success Stories

Example #1: Jason

Jason is a single forty-one-year old freelance graphic art designer. He would like to retire in another fifteen years when he is fifty-six. Because he is self-employed, he doesn't have a company pension plan. Disconcertingly, he hasn't started saving anything for retirement yet, either.

Makes no sense, you say. How can he possibly achieve his goal, given his financial situation? Wait a minute. Before you write Jason off as a hopeless dreamer, there are a few things you should know about him. First of all, he lives simply but well. He has always been adept at managing money. This means he could easily live a comfortable life on a modest retirement income of $26,000 a year (in today's dollars).

Another factor in his favor is the fact he has no debts. His house is fully paid for. He's also not carrying any credit card balances, car loans or other outstanding bills. Saving money for his retirement will be no problem, as his paycheque is all disposable income.

After carefully weighing the pros and cons, Jason decided to invest his retirement savings outside an RRSP. He did so for two reasons.

First of all, he won't have to count this money as part of his taxable income. That's because he has already paid tax on this money when he earned it. This will keep his income taxes low when he is retired. He'll get to keep most of his retirement money, rather than returning a large share to the federal government.

Second, he expects his retirement income will be modest. This makes him eligible for a larger OAS payment, which works out to an extra $385 a month in GIS benefits (in today's dollars) when he turns sixty-five. The extra money he stands to get will make a big difference in how much he needs to save.

Before we go any further, we should caution you that saving money outside an RRSP is not necessarily the right solution for everyone. Be sure to assess your own tax situation before you go this route. But this may be the way to go if you think your retirement income will be modest.

Worksheet 3 summarizes Jason's sources of retirement income, other than his own personal savings. You will notice that for the first four years of his retirement, Jason has no outside sources of income. This means he will need to rely entirely on his own savings.

The situation improves once he turns sixty as he can begin collecting CPP benefits. Once he turns sixty-five he is eligible to collect $857 per month (in today's dollars) in OAS and GIS benefits. This money is a bonus as it is not taxable income.

Worksheet 3: Jason's Sources of Retirement Income Other Than Personal Savings

Projected Retirement Date	Age	Work Pension	CPP	OAS/ GIS	Total Monthly Income	Total Annual Income
2020	56	$0			$0	$0
2021	57	$0			$0	$0
2022	58	$0			$0	$0
2023	59	$0			$0	$0
2024	60	$0	$350		$350	$4,200
2025	61	$0	$350		$350	$4,200
2026	62	$0	$350		$350	$4,200
2027	63	$0	$350		$350	$4,200
2028	64	$0	$350		$350	$4,200
2029	65	$0	$350	$857	$1,207	$14,484

Worksheet 4 looks at how much money Jason needs to save.

Worksheet 4: How Much Jason Needs to Save

Projected Retirement Date	Age	Total Annual Retirement Income	Projected Gross Income Needed	Personal Savings Needed
2020	56		$26,000	$26,000
2021	57		$26,000	$26,000
2022	58		$26,000	$26,000
2023	59		$26,000	$26,000
2024	60	$4,200	$26,000	$22,000
2025	61	$4,200	$26,000	$22,000
2026	62	$4,200	$26,000	$22,000
2027	63	$4,200	$26,000	$22,000
2028	64	$4,200	$26,000	$22,000
2029-2044	65-80	$14,500	$26,000	$11,500/year

Note that all figures are in today's dollars and that numbers have been rounded.

Jason estimates he will need about $386,500 in personal savings in order to retire when he is fifty-six. He got this amount by adding up how much he needs to top up his pension benefits out of his own pocket each year, until the age of eighty.

However, he quickly realized he doesn't really need to save this much. That's because of the power of compound interest. His money continues to grow, even after he starts drawing on it when he is retired. To be on the safe side, Jason assumes his savings will grow at a modest rate of three percent. He figures he needs roughly about $300,000.

Jason has made two assumptions in determining how much money he needs. First, his money will only have to last until he is eighty. At that time he intends to sell his house and move into a small apartment or senior's retirement centre. By then he reasons he will be ready for a break from yard work and home maintenance. The money he pockets from the sale can be used to top up his pension income.

Second, he intends to use up his capital investment, rather than live off the interest it generates, allowing him to save less than he would need otherwise.

Using an interest calculator he found on the Internet, Jason estimates that he will have to save $1,325 a month for the next fifteen years. This assumes a modest interest rate of three percent on his savings. If interest rates go up, he can save less each month, or continue to save the same amount and reach his early retirement savings goal faster.

Sure. You are probably thinking that saving $1,325 a month seems like a lot. That's because it is. But don't forget Jason is debt-free and has no children. This amount is equivalent to less than the average mortgage and car payment many people are making. He's willing to forgo some discretionary spending because the payoff will be worth it.

Did you notice that Jason could still retire early even though his savings are earning a low rate of return? This only goes to show that you don't need to count on high returns. This is true even if you start saving late.

What about inflation? Over half of Jason's retirement income will come from federal government pension cheques by the time he is sixty-five. Don't forget these are regularly adjusted for inflation. He has also prudently built a contingency fund into his projected annual expenses.

Keep in mind that if interest rates rise above three percent after he retires—and chances are good they will at some point over the twenty-five plus years of his retirement—his retirement nest egg will earn more than he projected. This means it will last longer. He can use the extra cash to top up any shortfalls in his budget. His best bet against inflation, though, is his simple debt-free lifestyle.

Example #2: Jennifer and Calvin

Jennifer and Calvin plan on retiring in eight years when they are fifty-six and fifty-eight. Calvin will not qualify for a full pension when he plans to quit his job and take early retirement. He hasn't been at his job long enough. Jennifer has been working part-time since the kids were small, and has no plans to go back to full-time work.

They've spent several evenings sitting around their kitchen table over numerous cups of coffee, carefully going over their expenses. They are confident they can have a comfortable retirement on $32,000 a year (in today's dollars). This should easily cover their basic expenses, and still leave them enough money to satisfy their passion to travel. Mind you, they do it on the cheap and rarely stay at four-star hotels.

What's the point of retiring, they reason, if they can't afford to have any fun? As soon as they hand in their notices, they plan on doing some extensive travelling in Argentina. This is something they have talked about for years, and are eagerly looking forward to sightseeing in Buenos Aires, touring local vineyards, and trekking in the Patagonian mountains.

Worksheets 3A and *3B* shows each of their individual sources of retirement income, while *Worksheet 3C* shows their combined retirement income.

Jennifer's Benefits

Worksheet 3A summarizes Jennifer's sources of retirement income. Although Jennifer doesn't qualify for a work pension, she will collect a modest CPP benefit of three hundred dollars a month (in today's dollars) when she turns sixty.

She also qualifies for a federal government OAS Allowance benefit of seventy-three dollars a month (in today's dollars) for two years, when she is sixty-three and sixty-four. Once she is sixty-five she begins collecting her full Old Age Security benefit of $472 a month (in today's dollars).

Admittedly, their prospects for early retirement look pretty dismal judging by Jennifer's finances alone.

Worksheet 3A: Jennifer's Sources of Retirement Income Other Than Personal Savings

Projected Retirement Date	Age	Work Pension	CPP	OAS Benefits	Total Monthly Income	Total Annual Income
2013	56				$0	$0
2014	57				$0	$0
2015	58				$0	$0
2016	59				$0	$0
2017	60		$300		$300	$3,600
2018	61		$300		$300	$3,600
2019	62		$300		$300	$3,600
2020	63		$300	$73	$373	$4,476
2021	64		$300	$73	$373	$4,476
2022	65		$300	$472	$772	$9,264

Note that all the amounts are in today's dollars. Also, for the sake of simplicity when calculating the value of annual benefits, we are assuming that both Jennifer and Calvin have birthdays in January.

Calvin's Benefits

Calvin is eligible for a partial work pension of just over one thousand dollars a month, or about thirteen thousand dollars a year. He will get another four hundred dollars a month in CPP benefits when he is sixty, and $627 a month in OAS benefits once he turns sixty-five. This goes down to $472 once Jennifer also begins collecting OAS monies, when she turns sixty-five, as their income will be too high to get the additional OAS supplement.

Worksheet 3B: Calvin's Sources of Retirement Income Other Than Personal Savings

Projected Retirement Date	Age	Work Pension	CPP	OAS Benefits	Total Monthly Income	Total Annual Income
2013	58	$1,100			$1,100	$13,200
2014	59	$1,100			$1,100	$13,200
2015	60	$1,100	$400		$1,500	$18,000
2016	61	$1,100	$400		$1,500	$18,000
2017	62	$1,100	$400		$1,500	$18,000
2018	63	$1,100	$400		$1,500	$18,000
2019	64	$1,100	$400		$1,500	$18,000
2020	65	$1,100	$400	$627	$2,127	$25,524

Note these amounts are all in today's dollars.

Jennifer and Calvin's Combined Benefits

Reassuringly, their financial situation turns around when Jennifer and Calvin add up their individual sources of income.

Worksheet 3C: Jennifer and Calvin's Sources of Retirement Income Other Than Personal Savings

Projected Retirement Date	Age	Work Pension	CPP	OAS Benefits	Total Monthly Income	Total Annual Income
2013	56/58	$1,100			$1,100	$13,200
2014	57/59	$1,100			$1,100	$13,200
2015	58/60	$1,100	$400		$1,500	$18,000
2016	59/61	$1,100	$400		$1,500	$18,000
2017	60/62	$1,100	$700		$1,800	$21,600
2018	61/63	$1,100	$700		$1,800	$21,600
2019	62/64	$1,100	$700		$1,800	$21,600
2020	63/65	$1,100	$700	$700	$2,500	$30,000
2021	64/66	$1,100	$700	$700	$2,500	$30,000
2022	65/67	$1,100	$700	$944	$2,744	$32,928

Their only source of income for the first two years of their retirement is Calvin's partial work pension of $1,100 a month. Once Calvin turns sixty they will receive another four hundred dollars a month from his CPP benefits. By 2017 they get seven hundred dollars a month in CPP payments when Jennifer begins collecting her CPP monies. By 2022 all of their retirement income comes from work and federal government pension benefits! The good news is that they are getting almost one thousand dollars more each year than they projected they would need.

Worksheet 4 looks at how much they need to save.

Worksheet 4: How Much Jennifer and Calvin Need to Save

Projected Retirement Date	Age	Total Annual Retirement Income	Projected Annual Expenses	Personal Savings Needed
2013	56/58	$13,200	$32,000	$19,000
2014	57/59	$13,200	$32,000	$19,000
2015	58/60	$18,000	$32,000	$14,000
2016	59/61	$18,000	$32,000	$14,000
2017	60/62	$21,600	$32,000	$11,000
2018	61/63	$21,600	$32,000	$11,000
2019	62/64	$21,600	$32,000	$11,000
2020	63/65	$30,000	$32,000	$2,000
2021	64/66	$30,000	$32,000	$2,000
2022	65/67	$32,928	$32,000	0

While Jennifer and Calvin initially need about nineteen thousand dollars out of their own pocket for the first two years of their retirement, the amount quickly goes down the older that they get. By the time Jennifer is sixty-five and Calvin is sixty-seven they don't need to chip in a cent of their own savings!

Believe it or not, the total amount they need to save is around $103,000. They arrived at this figure by adding up the shortfall in their income each year. Most retirement planners would naturally assume they missed a zero in their calculations. Of course, $103,000 is the bottom line. They could always save more if they were concerned about leaving themselves more of a financial cushion.

Another factor some people may want to consider is OAS benefits. It's best not to count them as part of your retirement income if you are worried about them. Why stress yourself out? Consider them a pleasant bonus when you get them. Of course, don't forget that you will have to save more to account for the shortfall in your retirement income if you decide to go this route.

Some of you may be wondering about inflation. Granted, prices will go up. However, Jennifer and Calvin can easily minimize how much they are affected if they keep their spending under control. Also keep in mind that their federal government benefits make up almost sixty percent of their total retirement income. Calvin's work pension makes up the rest. This means all of their retirement income is indexed for inflation by 2022.

Figuring Out Your Situation

It's time to get started and get some answers to your own situation. There's no need to worry. It's pretty simple. Basically, you have to find out the answers to two questions.

First of all, how much money will you get from work and government pension benefits? Second, how much do you need to save? Most people will have a gap between their projected retirement expenses and their retirement income. The difference is how much they need to save.

Worksheet 3 summarizes the different sources of retirement income you can expect to get. At this point, you are only looking at your work pension, if you have one, and government pension programs. Once you know how much you can get from these sources, and when you can get them, it's easy to figure out how much to save.

Get out some paper and make three copies of *Worksheet 3*. The first is for you, the second is for your partner, and the third is to record your combined income. You can skip the extra copies if you are on your own.

Start by filling it out on your own for now. This step makes it easier to figure out the tax implications of your retirement income, and help you strategically plan your savings. After all, there's no point in seeing your money needlessly taxed away, is there?

Fill in the year that you would like to retire at, and your age at that time. Continue filling in the years until you are sixty-five. Now record the different amounts from the various retirement benefits you are eligible for. When you are finished filling out *Worksheet 3*, you will have a good picture of your financial situation in retirement. Don't worry if the numbers look small.

Use the third copy of *Worksheet 3* to combine the information that you and your partner individually recorded. Start with the year you would like to retire at and your ages. Now add up your income for each income source to get your total household income when you are retired.

Put your individual worksheets aside for now. You will need to look at them again when you read Chapter Eight.

Worksheet 3: Sources of Retirement Income Other Than Personal Savings

Projected Retirement Date	Your Age	Work Pension	CPP Benefits	OAS Benefits	Total Monthly Income	Total Annual Income

How are you doing? Maybe you are in the enviable position of not needing to save a cent of your own money. Don't feel bad if this doesn't apply to you. Few people are so lucky.

How Much Do You Need to Save?

You're now ready for *Worksheet 4*. Fill out *Worksheet 4* together if you are married or living with a partner.

Worksheet 4 will provide you with an estimate of how much money you need to save. Start by filling in the year and age columns, starting at the year you anticipate retiring, until the year you and your partner are at least both sixty-five.

Fill in your total household monthly income from *Worksheet 3*. Next, add your annual living expenses from *Worksheet 2* in Chapter Four.

You're now ready to figure out how much you need to save. You don't need any fancy computer programs. The calculation just involves simple subtraction, or the difference between your projected expenses and your retirement income. The amount should go down the older that you get. Keep in mind that you will be getting your maximum federal government retirement benefits by the time you are sixty-five.

A Word of Advice

We should caution you. Go over the numbers again and double-check them, as you get closer to retirement. You can appreciate that it is better to identify a funding shortfall while you are working. It is a fairly simple task to increase the amount you save, or postpone retirement for a year or two.

The alternative could be a little awkward. You might feel sheepish if you make this discovery after handing in your notice, telling the boss what you think of him, and then coming back months later frantically begging for your job back.

Worksheet 4: How Much Do You Need to Save?

Projected Retirement Date	Your Age	Projected Annual Costs of Retirement	Total Annual Retirement Income	Personal Savings Needed

You now know how much savings you will need. Will it be enough? Too much? Chapter Seven outlines four strategies that you can consider to answer this question.

7:

Four Strategies for Saving

In the last chapter you calculated a ballpark figure of how much you need to save. Is it enough? Too much? Not sure? These are good questions. How much do you actually need to save, and how do you do it?

Let's get back to Jennifer and Calvin for a minute. When they first began planning their retirement, they discovered that there is more than one way to figure out how much money to save. They are bright and articulate and came up with four strategies with no trouble. Each strategy gives them a different estimate, which affects how much they need to save.

Before we get started, we should let you know that Jennifer and Calvin only recently started saving for their retirement. They would like to retire in eight years. No doubt retirement planning experts would tell them they are foolish, and their dreams are completely hopeless.

We're willing to bet they can do it. For one thing, they have the self-discipline. They are willing to make some personal sacrifices, trim their expenses, and forgo small pleasures. They know that a daily double mocha cappuccino, expensive restaurant meals, and weekly shopping trips to designer boutiques won't come close to making up for missing out on their early retirement dream. It's easy to stay focused.

The four strategies they came up with are outlined below.

1. Be the richest folks in the nursing home.
2. Die broke but happy.
3. Save for a rainy day.
4. Scale down expenses.

Strategy #1: Richest Folks in the Nursing Home

This strategy wasn't hard to dream up. It is based on conventional thinking, and is the plan of action most retirement planners favor. Under this strategy, you save a large pile of money and live off the interest it generates. In the meantime you preserve your capital as an inheritance for your grateful children, favorite niece, or pet charities when you die.

To make it easier to follow along, the information from Worksheet 4 shows how deeply Jennifer and Calvin have to dig into their own pockets each year to finance their early retirement. You'll remember these numbers from the previous chapter.

Worksheet 4: How Much Jennifer and Calvin Need to Save

Projected Retirement Date	Age	Total Annual Retirement Income	Projected Annual Expenses	Personal Savings Needed
2013	56/58	$13,200	$32,000	$19,000
2014	57/59	$13,200	$32,000	$19,000
2015	58/60	$18,000	$32,000	$14,000
2016	59/61	$18,000	$32,000	$14,000
2017	60/62	$21,600	$32,000	$11,000
2018	61/63	$21,600	$32,000	$11,000
2019	62/64	$21,600	$32,000	$11,000
2020	63/65	$29,856	$32,000	$2,000
2021	64/66	$29,856	$32,000	$2,000
2022	65/67	$32,928	$32,000	0

So how much do they need to save? Jennifer and Calvin calculated they would need a $475,000 pool of capital to generate annual returns of nineteen thousand dollars. This assumes a modest four percent rate of return. Most retirement planners would have Jennifer and Calvin saving even more.

The nineteen thousand dollars their nest egg earns each year will easily cover their expenses for the first two years of their retirement, and provide them with a healthy surplus in later years.

For obvious reasons, Jennifer and Calvin quickly discarded this strategy. Saving almost half a million dollars is completely unrealistic, especially given their short savings timeframe. Where will they get it?

There is an even more convincing reason not to go this route. They don't need this much money. The amount of personal savings they require each year drops, as they get older. By the time Jennifer is sixty-five, they don't need any personal savings at all. That's because federal government pension cheques pick up the slack, easily allowing them to meet their target retirement income.

If they followed the "Richest Folks in the Nursing Home" strategy, they would find themselves with an income of $52,000 (in today's dollars) in 2022. They only need $32,000 (in today's dollars) in order to live well.

Why get stressed out saving more than they require, they reasoned? They'd have trouble spending it all. Besides, the extra money just means they'll wind up paying more income tax on their earnings.

As they saw it, they'd be burning the midnight oil, scrimping and saving while they were young, just so they could give it back to the government when they got old! It didn't sound like a very good incentive to them.

Strategy #2: Dying Broke but Happy

When Jennifer and Calvin added up the shortfall in their income each year, they calculated the amount they need to save is about $103,000. Now this is more like it.

In short, how this strategy works is simple. They would dip into their principal each year. By 2022, when their pension income meets their expenses, their savings nest egg would be almost cleaned out. They still have their house, they reasoned, and could always sell it if they were desperate for cash. They would literally die broke, but happy.

Strategy #3: Saving For A Rainy Day

Jennifer and Calvin are financially conservative by nature. Realistically, they know all they need to save is around $103,000. Yet, they don't feel comfortable with having just enough. They want more of a financial cushion. For their own peace of mind, they calculated they have to save around $150,000. This provides them with a modest amount of "extra" money in case they need it.

Under this strategy, Jennifer and Calvin draw down their principal until the year 2017. By this time, they only need about two thousand dollars of their own savings to meet their retirement expenses.

By 2017 their RRSP savings will be roughly valued at just over seventy thousand dollars. This is based on a modest three percent interest rate. This will easily generate the two thousand dollars they need, meeting their income requirements for the next two years.

After 2019, their investment will provide them with a modest surplus of two thousand dollars a year, and for every year after that. This money is a bonus. That's because their income from their work and government pensions effortlessly covers their living costs. Of course, if interest rates go up, the returns on their investment will be even higher.

A great plan. But how do they save $150,000? Don't forget they only have eight years to do it. Fortunately, their house is paid for, they've already put aside money for their children's education, and they don't have any large debts.

They realize they'll have to make some sacrifices. It won't always be easy but they are prepared to do what it takes. Their early retirement dream takes precedence over luxuries, or spending on extras they don't really need.

Assuming a three percent interest rate, they figure they will have to save $1,400 a month, for the next eight years.

While Jennifer and Calvin like this option, they realized there is an easier way to finance their retirement. All they have to do is downsize their lifestyle, as in Strategy #4.

Strategy #4: Scaling Down Expenses

Jennifer and Calvin have a large house worth $220,000. Once the kids are gone, they won't need all that space. In fact, they already resent the time it takes to clean and maintain it, let alone pay for exorbitant—and rising— utility bills.

They plan to sell their house once they retire and move into a smaller one. It wasn't a hard decision to make. Reasoning that they can buy a smaller one worth $150,000 (in today's dollars), they will still have a windfall of at least fifty thousand dollars once they deduct real estate fees, legal costs and other expenses. This means they only need to save $100,000 in order to have the $150,000 nest egg they have set as their savings goal.

Best of all, they won't have to scrimp and save. If they put aside one thousand dollars a month for the next eight years, they will easily reach, and surpass, their savings goal.

Naturally, the interest rate is only three percent, as they know they don't need to count on high returns to finance their retirement. If interest rates go up, it's a bonus.

Figuring Out Your Own Strategy

You need to add up the numbers for your own situation, and your own comfort level. How much of a cushion do you need? There are no hard and fast rules as the amount varies from person to person.

A big factor, of course, is the lifestyle you expect to have in retirement. If you're a "shop-until-you-drop-consumer" and you can't live without a daily trip to the mall, you will have to save more.

Don't forget that there is a downside to all this spending. The simple fact is expect to work longer. You may even have to give up your early retirement dream altogether. Is all that spending worth it?

If you're serious about retiring early, it's crucial to get your spending under control right now. Think of it this way. If you live frugally now, and curb a lot of frivolous and unnecessary spending, you'll be used to a simpler lifestyle by the time you retire. You won't need as much to live on.

What's more, you'll have learned a valuable lesson in money management. It's not complicated, and certainly not rocket science, but still something most people forget. Namely, stop wasting your money on lots of little things that don't matter. Save your money for the big things that do. That's the only way you are going to realize your dreams.

What are you waiting for? Get started now. If you keep making excuses, and you are not prepared to find the time and make the commitment, you are never going to be able to retire early.

Start your research, and work through the numbers for your own situation. Try out various strategies. Perhaps a choice you never considered before means fewer savings and an earlier retirement date for you.

Have you noticed that the amount you need to save is far less than the wildly exaggerated amounts retirement ads and brochures would have you believe you need?

Early retirement now becomes a real possibility.

8:

Tax Planning Doesn't Have to be Taxing

It's funny how people lie awake at night obsessing about the wrong things. They toss and turn in a cold sweat anxiously thinking about how to come up with that million they need, short of robbing a bank.

Stop worrying. Instead of losing sleep wondering how to build up your wealth, think about something more mundane instead—your income taxes. At least this is something you can realistically do something about.

What's the point in earning and saving money if you have to give most of it away? It makes more sense to think of ways to trim your retirement tax bill.

If your financial situation is fairly straightforward, you should be able to figure this out on your own. The other alternative is to establish a good working relationship with a knowledgeable tax accountant. In fact, if your finances are fairly complicated, take him out for coffee now and then and make him a good friend. His advice could save you a substantial pile of cash.

Take advantage of all the tax rules you can. Obviously, you need to know about them first, so become informed and stay on top of things because rules change. That's why it is important to read the financial pages of newspapers or talk to an accountant and keep up on the latest information. It would be a shame to miss out on deductions you are eligible for.

There are many tax strategies for reducing your income taxes, but many apply only if you are in a high income bracket. The following are some simple strategies to consider if you have a more modest income. The list isn't exhaustive by any means, but it's enough to get you started.

Income Splitting

One way to reduce your taxable income is to split your income as evenly as you can between you and your partner. The idea is to take maximum advantage of lower tax brackets. Two simple ways of income splitting are:

> ➢ Spousal RRSPs.
> ➢ CPP Retirement Benefits.

Spousal RRSPs

These are an effective means of income splitting if one partner is in a higher tax bracket and the income of the other partner is much lower. The following example will give you an idea of how this works.

When Jennifer and Calvin were first planning their retirement, they decided to buy most of their RRSPs in Jennifer's name. This was a smart tax move on their part. Jennifer's retirement income will be considerably lower than Calvin's, as she does not qualify for a work pension. During the first few years of their retirement, when they expect to rely heavily on their own savings, Jennifer can claim most of their RRSP income. Calvin will claim the income from his work pension, in effect splitting their taxable income between the two of them.

CPP Retirement Benefits

If you are collecting CPP retirement benefits, and your partner is at least sixty years old, you are allowed to transfer half of your CPP retirement benefit to your partner. This strategy is especially effective if your partner is not eligible to receive any CPP benefits. Take advantage of this if you can. You can reduce the amount you have to claim by half.

It's also effective if one partner has a much higher income than the other. Tax rules allow you to assign half your CPP benefits to the lower earning partner. Keep in mind that your partner must assign the same percentage of their benefits back to you. The net effect is that you claim fewer benefits and your partner claims more. You have effectively split your total CPP income between the two of you.

Federal Exemptions

Another advantage to getting older is that you are allowed to claim more tax exemptions. On top of your basic exemptions, you also become eligible for age-related exemptions, which reduce your taxable income even further. Some of the federal exemptions are:

Federal Tax Exemptions for 2004

Federal Exemption	Amount
Basic Federal Exemption	$8,012
Spouse or Common-law Partner Amount	$7,484
Pension Income Exemption	$1,000
Age 65 Exemption	$3,912

The pension income amount refers to retirement income you receive from sources other than government benefits. This includes money from a private pension, an annuity, a registered retirement income fund or a life income fund.

You are allowed to transfer certain non-refundable tax credits to your spouse. This reduces the federal taxes they have to pay. For example, if one spouse has a low income and doesn't need the tax credits, they can transfer these credits to their spouse who has a higher income. Transferable amounts include the age sixty-five amount and the pension income amount.

Don't forget that each province also has its own tax exemptions. Make sure you are aware of what these are and take advantage of them.

You'll need to work through your own tax situation. The idea is to lower your taxable retirement income as much as possible. We have mentioned a few simple ways to do this. Don't just rely on our word, though. Research other options so that you don't lose out on any other deductions you might be eligible for.

9:

Taking Control of Your Fears

By now you understand the wealth management industry, and know it is largely driven by self-interest. Naturally you don't harbour any hard feelings. Financial advisors are just trying to make a living, like everyone else. You're also aware of the seven retirement myths that are in their best interests to perpetuate. You may even have worked through the exercises and done the math. You know how much money you need, what you need to save, and where it is going to come from.

Congratulations! You are well on the way to succeeding in your early retirement plans. So why the heck are you still sitting here? Why aren't you doing anything more about your situation? What's holding you back? Are the following fears stopping you from pursuing your dreams?

> ➢ You're scared of making a mistake.
> ➢ You're afraid of losing your identity.
> ➢ You're afraid of giving up your full pension.
> ➢ You're afraid you will have a reduced standard of living.

Scared of Making a Mistake

No one wants to look like a fool. That's why we bring in an expert to tell us what to do. Everything is so complicated these days. You can hardly expect the average person to know what to do and not make a complete mess of the job.

Besides who has the time? That's why a lucrative service industry has evolved to do the jobs we used to do ourselves. Nowadays we have experts who clean our carpets, de-clutter our homes, walk our dogs, arrange dinner parties, or even shop for us.

That's too bad. Sure we save time. But at a personal cost, as we've undermined our self-confidence. These days few people are brave and energetic enough to figure out what to do on their own any more, or even to think independently. It's gotten to the point where we rely on experts to tell us how to live.

Financial experts tell us we need to be rich to retire. The only way to achieve our goal is to invest in stocks or mutual funds, and hope our returns deliver a steady ten percent or more. We risk spending our old age on the bread line, or a burden to our relatives, if we ignore their advice. There's no one to blame but ourselves if our money runs out before we do.

Human resources consultants tell us that professional success and fulfillment comes from moving up the career ladder. In order to get there—and even after we have arrived—we have to work long, exhausting hours and trade off our family for our job. The payoff at the end is the "golden handshake" and full pension.

Economists tell us it's our civic duty to keep spending. It doesn't matter if we can't afford it. Shopping keeps the economy growing and ensures everyone has jobs. There's no incentive to conserve resources, and our money. After all, who wants to be responsible for throwing someone out on the street?

The advertising industry has tapped our insecurities. They know our self-esteem and self-worth are wrapped up in what we own. Ads bombard us with admonitions to buy things we never knew we needed. We are raised to believe money buys happiness.

So what's the bottom line? The fact is, we've forgotten how to think for ourselves. We can't be trusted to do even the most mundane tasks anymore without a high-priced expert. It's gotten so bad that we've let others define what success is. Can you think of any other reason why we accept the insane lives most people lead these days?

Conventional wisdom dictates that we work long hours if we want to get ahead. That's why people willingly plug away at the office from sunup to sundown. It's the only way to get on the fast track, advance our careers, live in upscale neighbourhoods, and send our kids to good middle class schools. Naturally, we need two or more expensive cars parked in the driveway. How else can we get to our jobs to pay for it all?

The average person is struggling under staggering levels of debt. We have been conditioned to think of this as normal. It's just the price you pay to live the life you think you need.

There's no let up to the pressure. We have to keep running just to stand still, in order to maintain a lifestyle we can't afford. If we are lucky, we can eventually abandon the rat race and retire one day. This assumes the stress doesn't give us a heart attack before then.

Most people end up paying a high price for blindly accepting conventional standards of success. Their obsession with getting ahead, and the kind of lifestyle it buys, doesn't provide a lot of satisfaction or fulfillment. It's a wonder more people haven't said enough is enough. They're going to stop running with the herd. They've come to realize the herd is headed in the wrong direction anyway.

Your options are seriously limited if you only do what everyone else is doing. That's because there is only one "right" way of doing things. The problem is that it's not going to be right for you. When was the last time a one-size-fits-all t-shirt actually looked flattering on you?

You are not lazy, or lack ambition, if you abandon the career ladder and retire early. You are not shirking your civic duty if you jump off the consumer bandwagon. On the contrary, you are just deciding what success means on your own terms. You're determining your own lifestyle, and setting your own pace for a change. Think of it as being brave, not foolhardy.

Forget the doom and gloom warnings of retirement experts. You're not condemned to living in the back of your van in your old age if you ignore their advice. Remember, you're making your own rules and doing what's right for you.

So what if you don't have the pile of money the experts say is absolutely essential? You don't need it. So what if you still have faith in public pensions? You're not being hopelessly naive and unsophisticated, as they'd have you believe. Besides, you know the experts have a vested interest in being unduly pessimistic.

If you've done your retirement planning right, you can quit on your own terms. There's no reason why you have to base your future on cookie-cutter financial advice. Don't be afraid of making a mistake. Keep in mind that you are doing what's right for you.

Losing Your Identity

An article about young adults in their early twenties, and their idealistic career ambitions, made us stop and think. In North America we tend to confuse our job with our life, and who we are. That's because we put an unrealistic emphasis on our careers.

Don't you think it's time we readjusted our priorities? It is a lot healthier to view our job as a way to pay the bills—so that we can get a life. With any luck you enjoy what you do. But your job shouldn't define who you are.

Personally, we can't imagine there are too many jobs out there that are going to provide us with all the personal fulfillment, satisfaction, intellectual stimulation and excitement that we want in life. Sure, a lucky few may have their personal goals met through their job. But the rest of us have to keep looking.

In our obsession with getting ahead, we size people up by their paycheque and how prestigious their job is. The pinnacle of success is when you have climbed your way up the career ladder to the top. Conventional wisdom would have you believe a status job, fancy corner office, private secretary, generous expense account and fat paycheque are your just awards for all the sacrifices you have made to get there.

Do you ever wonder if the sacrifices are worth it? Long hours are expected and, in fact, are a normal part of our work culture these days. People are tied to their cell phones and laptops, even on weekends. They take pride in the fact they don't take vacations anymore. Crazy, isn't it? You wouldn't brag about a heroin addiction. Why would you brag about a work addiction?

Surveys have found that the hours of work are getting back to those of industrial workers back in the mid-19th century. Back then, sweatshops with twelve-hour days, running full throttle six days a week, were a routine occurrence. These appalling conditions led to the first wave of workplace reforms.

Instead of going forward, we're regressing to a less progressive period in our history. Downsizing, plant closures and corporate and government belt tightening have no doubt played a large part in our current restructuring.

There is a downside to this kind of corporate culture. Your job is literally who you are. If you don't work, who are you? No wonder retirement is a terrifying thought for many people. When you quit your job you lose your identify. It is even more terrifying if you don't have any hobbies, interests or social connections outside work.

Are you one of these people? Is the fear of losing your identity holding you back from pursuing your dream of early retirement?

Don't feel bad. You are not alone. An astonishing number of people feel bewildered once they no longer have an office to go to. This is true even if their job was unbelievably tedious and mind numbing.

Don't you think it is time to re-evaluate who you are? Many people could slow down if they wanted to. They're just not willing to make less money. Sadly, their identity is closely tied to the size of their paycheque. That's a mistake. With their status gone, it's a sure bet they're headed for a miserable retirement.

Don't wait until you retire to get a real life. You need one now. Besides, if you wait too long, it might be too late. You may never get a second chance, especially if you develop serious health problems in middle age.

Giving Up a Full Pension

The other day we ran into a former neighbour whom we hadn't seen in a long time. He was on stress leave from a demanding job. Nevertheless, he was determined to go back once his leave was up. After all, he just had another five years before he could quit and collect his full pension. From a financial standpoint, it didn't make sense. He has no kids, his house is paid for, and he's been putting aside money into retirement savings for years.

It astounds us how many otherwise intelligent and successful people are horrified at the thought of giving up a penny of their pension. It's funny how they can be stressed out, depressed and popping pills to make it through the day—or suffering heart palpitations and migraine headaches. Yet, when you suggest they think about leaving, they are incredulous. "Why? I've only got a few more years left to go."

They are going to pay a high price for their short sightedness. Money won't do you any good if you're not around to enjoy it.

Too often we forget that life is precious. Why squander it and stick around at a job that's destroying your health? Can you think of a good reason for staying? Don't make the mistake of letting the company pension plan kill you and your dreams. You could be making far more sacrifices than you need to. The benefits probably aren't worth the price you're paying anyway.

Even if you are in good health, or love your job, what are you gaining from working until you qualify for a full pension? Sure you will get some more money. What else will you get? Have you thought about what you are giving up—two or more years of your life that you could otherwise be spending with your family, pursuing hobbies and interests, and just plain old enjoying life? Have you taken the time to:

> ➢ Find out the work pension benefits you are eligible for if you were to quit right now?
> ➢ Calculate how much money you need to live in retirement?
> ➢ Look at what your other income sources are?
> ➢ Think of ways you could cut back your expenses?

Don't just sit back and complain. You will never make any changes in your life that way. There's no easy way around it, you have to make the effort. You could discover that you don't need a full pension, and still have a comfortable lifestyle.

So what's holding you back?

Reducing Your Standard of Living

Most people are firmly convinced that you need lots of money to have a happy retirement. Having read the book this far, you know this isn't true. Sadly, many people have given up any dreams of early retirement because their personal financial situation seems like an insurmountable obstacle.

Retirement planning kits perpetuate the myth of money and happiness. Retired couples are shown lounging on a cruise ship sipping margaritas, or teeing off at a ritzy country club. No wonder you need lots of cash. At least far more than if you stayed home growing prize tulips, or puttering around your garage workshop.

As long as you can meet your basic needs, the secret to a happy retirement isn't money. We'll bet if you talked to happily retired couples, they wouldn't proudly pull out their financial portfolio and tell you about all their blue chip investments. Most would talk about the activities they are involved in.

Don't make the mistake of thinking that just because you are no longer being paid, you don't need to be busy in a meaningful way. Doing something you enjoy keeps your mind active, and you get satisfaction from doing something worthwhile.

Are you afraid of retiring because you think you don't have enough money to have a happy retirement? Sure, you will need enough money to meet your basic needs. But the answer to a happy retirement isn't that simple. The bigger question you have to answer is what do you want to be doing now that you no longer have the structure of work to fill your day.

So, what's holding you back from pursuing your dreams?

10:

Before Storming Into the Boss's Office

We don't know if you have seen the movie, *Lost in America*. It's the story of two fast-track New Yorkers who are fed up with their stressed out lives. One day they impulsively decide to leave the rat race behind for good. They quit their jobs, buy an RV and set out on a journey of self-discovery across America.

Not long after they leave, they end up losing all their money in Las Vegas. While the husband is fast asleep in their hotel room, his wife feverishly works the roulette tables. She's trying to score some easy cash to finance their new life. Instead, she loses it all. Desperate, and forced to give up their trip, they end up living in a trailer park working at minimum wage jobs. This is quite a comedown for two former high-powered business executives.

Being a Hollywood movie, their odyssey ends on a somewhat happy note. They come to their senses and gratefully go back to their former stressed out lives, at lower pay.

While it's a funny movie, it also serves as a not so subtle warning. This is what can happen if you try something as rash as quitting your job, and searching out your dreams. Daring to do something unconventional questions the values most people unconditionally accept.

If there's a lesson to be learned, it's that you shouldn't just quit your job and hit the road. Retirement is a major life transition. You need to properly plan for it. Retirement can be the best years of your life, and you don't want to risk blowing it. The keys to a financially stress-free retirement are to:

- ➢ Plan ahead.
- ➢ Be conservative in your assumptions.
- ➢ Live within your means.

If you do your retirement planning right, there will rarely be a day when you're not smiling. There is no reason not to. Early retirement could be one of the best things you have ever done.

Planning Ahead

Don't take a stab in the dark and blindly guess about how much you need and where it will come from. For your own peace of mind, it is far better to be prepared. Know the answers to the following questions:

> ➤ How much money do you need to live on when you are retired?
> ➤ Where are you going to get the money?
> ➤ How much can you get from public pensions and a work pension, if you have one?
> ➤ How much personal savings do you need?

Do these questions sound familiar? If you have worked through the worksheets in this book, you should already have a pretty good picture of your finances, and how much you need to save to make it happen. It is less stressful to do this before you actually retire.

The big payoff to your research is the realization that early retirement can be a very real possibility. The other benefit, of course, is that you have a good idea of the return you will need on your investments to give you the savings you need.

Okay. So you've done the research, answered all the questions and got your plan in place. You're finished, right? Not quite, although give yourself a well-deserved pat on the back. You have done most of the hard work. Now you just need to review your plan on a regular basis.

Circumstances change. You might need to re-think your plan to account for these changes.

Things that could derail your retirement planning are the loss of your job—and the pension plan that went with it—divorce, unexpected expenses that mean you can't save as much, or the high cost of utilities and car insurance, which could throw off your projected retirement budget.

It doesn't mean you have to scrap your plans. Sit down and re-work the numbers. Perhaps you will have to save more, work a year or two longer, or re-think your budget.

Ideally, you should review your plan at least once a year, especially if you are close to retirement. Don't make the mistake of working through the numbers ten years before you plan on retiring, and then setting them aside until just before you retire. Or worse yet, only start planning the year before you retire. In that case, you could be in for a rude shock. Think of how discouraging it would be to find out you can't afford to retire because your finances are a mess.

Being Conservative in Your Assumptions

Most retired people will tell you it's best to be conservative in your assumptions, especially when it comes to money. One of the biggest mistakes potential retirees make is to count on high returns to finance their retirement. That's because of their misguided belief that they need a large nest egg. Are you one of these people?

You could find yourself in serious trouble if there is a downturn in the economy. What are you going to do if you are counting on ten percent returns, and you only get five percent?

Being a high roller can be stressful. There's nothing worse than discovering you have half the money you thought you would. Do you have enough money to tide you over until returns on your investments go back up—assuming they ever do—or they don't drop even further?

For your own peace of mind, we would caution you to plan your retirement around low returns on your savings. If you get more, it's a bonus. It's ludicrous to assume your investments will yield ten percent returns for the next thirty years, despite what retirement experts tell you. This doesn't sound much different than playing the roulette tables at Las Vegas.

There's another area it pays to be conservative. That's when you estimate your retirement budget. Make sure it is realistic, and then set aside enough money to comfortably live on. Otherwise you could find yourself a reluctant connoisseur of macaroni and cheese dinners in your old age. Don't make the mistake of assuming you can cut everything down to the bone once the kids are gone. While you want to avoid saving more than you need, don't underestimate your needs either. Be sure to allow for contingencies.

The best solution is to review your anticipated retirement budget every year to make sure it is realistic and on track. It's easier to do this before you actually retire, than to discover you grossly underestimated your living costs.

Living Within Your Means

Recently we received a brochure in the mail from a financial institution assuring us (along with thousands of others) that ready cash was just a phone call away. We could be approved for a loan within minutes, even if we had recently declared bankruptcy. There would be no annoying credit checks. Nor was there any need to supply personal financial statements, tax assessments or employment references. What a deal!

It's no surprise so many people are trapped under a spiraling mountain of debt. With terms like these, who can resist? Unfortunately, there's a flip side to easy credit that you're seldom told about. You have to keep working to maintain a lifestyle you can't afford. At this rate your early retirement dreams will never be more than pleasant thoughts.

Have you ever thought about why we're such voracious consumers? Are we trying to buy happiness? There is no denying that spending feels good. Besides, coveting our neighbour's wealth and wanting something better is as old as the Bible. We're just trying to keep up.

Our obsession with conspicuous consumption has a dark side. We miss the boat on what's really important. A house full of material possessions won't make up for a life that lacks any real joy or meaning.

Are you serious about retiring early? Then curb mindless spending. Keep your expenses low. Despite most people's emphasis on income, costs are more important than earnings. Think about it for a minute. What would you rather do? Control your spending? Or get a second job to make more money, so you can spend more? Why increase your stress level when there is an easier solution?

Most people can effortlessly cut back without any appreciable impact on their lifestyle. In fact, it would be an eye opener for most of us if we took an inventory of all the things we bought over the years, and didn't need.

Living a simple lifestyle while you are working is good practice for when you are retired. Jacqueline retired when she was in her early fifties. When she first started thinking about early retirement, she developed some good habits while she was still working. These have served her well now that she is older.

> ➢ Whenever she got a raise, she resisted escalating her lifestyle to match her new salary.
> ➢ She kept her fixed costs low.
> ➢ Once her mortgage was paid off, she didn't give in to the temptation to buy a bigger house or move to a "better" neighbourhood.

> She lives in an area that has excellent public transportation, so she has never had to rely on a car to get to work.

It's easy to get caught up in wanting more. The secret is to be happy with what you already have. Appreciate the intangibles, like close family and good friends. Most retirees will tell you these are more important than a large bank account anyway.

11:

Getting a Life

We don't want to leave you with the wrong impression. We've spent a lot of time talking about money. There's no denying you need some. You don't want to be dumpster diving in your old age.

But money is not the most important part of your retirement planning. In fact, we're willing to bet there is a direct correlation between a mid-life obsession with working and saving and an unhappy retirement.

We all know people like Mr. Busy Executive— hopefully he's not you, or your spouse—who think they can buy a happy retirement. Mr. Executive is in his fifties. He's overweight and a workaholic. He's usually off to the office at seven in the morning and working until well after seven at night.

In his single-minded obsession with working hard and advancing his career, he has traded off his wife and children for the office. He figures there's no need to worry. There will be plenty of time for them later, once he decides to abandon the rat race.

He's looking forward to being able to slow down the pace and relax in his golden years. He doesn't plan on quitting, though, until there is enough money in the bank to ensure an affluent retirement lifestyle. Judging by the punishing hours he's putting in, it looks like he's well on his way. He's managed to put together an enviable blue chip portfolio worth hundreds of thousands of dollars.

After a long and stressful day at the office, Mr. Executive is beat. He puts his feet up, watches some mindless TV, snacks on some junk food and throws back a couple of martinis every night.

Who needs to worry about hobbies? A big investment portfolio will take care of his retirement needs. After all, he can buy the lifestyle he wants. He's got the cash to golf at the ritziest country clubs, live in an exclusive retirement community and holiday at fancy resorts. This assumes, of course, he actually lives long enough to enjoy his hard-earned riches.

What Mr. Executive doesn't know is that he will be disappointed once he retires. His only passion in life is work. In fact, not to be too unkind, most people would describe him as pretty dull and uninteresting. That's predictable, given the fact he hasn't taken any steps to invest in himself, and has no hobbies or interests outside his job.

While a certain amount of money is important, it's not the key ingredient to a happy and fulfilling retirement. Most people get sidetracked, and spend too much time anxiously thinking about the wrong thing. Instead of worrying about how much money you need, spend some time thinking about the kinds of things you want to do. You would probably be surprised at how little money it takes to live a satisfying lifestyle.

Remember our retired couple, Mike and Helen, from Chapter Three? As you may recall, they are living on $24,000 a year. A lot of people would consider this a poverty level income. They would be amazed to discover their "jet set lifestyle". Last year Mike and Helen went to Spain and France, and the year before they visited the Queen Charlotte Islands. This year they're planning a trip to the Dominican Republic. According to Mike, people worry about money too much. Mike and Helen never worry, and still manage to have a good life.

Focusing on What's Important

Key ingredients for a good retirement are key ingredients for a good life right now. So what makes a good life? Most people would agree on the following—or something close to it—as characteristics of a good life, which is to be:

➢ Healthy,
➢ Physically fit,
➢ Happy,
➢ Have close social relationships with family and friends,
➢ Do things that are fulfilling, and
➢ Continually be learning new things and growing as a person.

Did you notice anything missing from the list? Wealth, of course, is conspicuously absent. Sure, we'd all love a big bank account. But intuitively we know that money alone is not going to make us happy. Look at all the miserable rich people who lead dysfunctional lives, commit suicide, drink themselves to death, or are drug addicts.

Let's get back to Mr. Busy Executive for a minute. He's well on his way to facing a life of emptiness and boredom when he's retired. The odds are stacked against him because he:

➢ Works too many long hours.
➢ Is too busy or tired to spend any time with his family.
➢ Has lost touch with his friends and makes little or no effort to make new ones.

- ➢ Hasn't shown an interest in anything other than his job for years.
- ➢ Eats a poor diet, most days grabbing something fast, usually high in fat and calories.
- ➢ Consumes far too much coffee.
- ➢ Drinks too much.
- ➢ Smokes excessively.
- ➢ Never has the time or energy to exercise.
- ➢ Is overweight.

Do you see yourself in any of this? If you do, it's time to take stock and re-evaluate your priorities in life. Do you really want to be old and reflect back on your life with regret? If you had to do it all over again, what would you do differently?

We spend far too much time thinking about our investments and not about the things that are really important. Not all wealth is measured by dollars or what's in our bank account.

Sure, it's nice to be able to buy what you want, when you want it. But at the end of the day, think about what's really important in your life.

Here's a list of what is important in our lives.

What's Important in Our Life

Important	Not Important
Good health	Big house
Loyal friends	Luxury car
Strong family relationships	Luxury cruises and nights at the opera
Hobbies and interests	Country club membership and joining the cocktail circuit
Enough money to comfortably live on	Big investment portfolio

Make your own list. What is important in your life? What isn't important? Where are you concentrating your energies?

Taking Care of Your Health

Taking care of your health is one of the most crucial things you can do to prepare for retirement. Your lifestyle choices will be harshly restricted if you are sick and frail.

While it is encouraging to know that life expectancies have been growing, according to statistics the average Canadian can expect to spend a decade or so in less than full health. It's a sobering reminder to stay active and take care of yourself.

Ask yourself these questions:

- ➢ Are you eating a nutritious well-balanced diet?
- ➢ Do you try to limit your fat intake?
- ➢ Do you smoke?
- ➢ Are you a moderate drinker?
- ➢ Do you exercise on a regular basis?
- ➢ Is your weight at a desired level for your age, sex and size?
- ➢ Are you able to cope with stress in your life?

While unusual, we read about an eighty-one year old retired businessman who joined a cycling group eight years ago. Since then, he regularly goes on forty kilometer rides twice a week. "If I didn't get regular exercise," he says, "I'd feel lousy."

By staying fit and active, you are doing your best to prolong your healthy years.

Hobbies and Interests

You don't want to retire and find yourself with too much time on your hands. Sure, when you're busy working, time seems like a luxury. When you are retired, you can only check your investments so often. What do you do next? Lying on the sofa watching re-runs on TV is okay for a while, but a steady diet can get terribly mind numbing. Unless you've got something meaningful to do every day, you'll soon wish you were back at work.

Unfortunately, most people don't have a clue. They plan on winging retirement. An instructor at a retirement seminar shared an anecdote with our class that really brought this home. He'd been asked to set up a program for seniors at a local mall.

Storeowners were up in arms because of a group of old men who were hanging around the mall all day. They were a harmless bunch. They idly sat on benches staring at shoppers as they went by. But that was the problem. They were scaring customers away.

The solution was simple. Obviously, they needed something to do. A job board was set up in a vacant room. This would be a place where the men could congregate, chat and have a free coffee and donut, and make themselves useful volunteering to do whatever odd job needed to be done.

We'll bet these seniors never imagined they'd end up hanging around a mall, for lack of anything else to do, when they were dreaming of their retirement.

Make a list of all the things you want to do once you are no longer working. Put the things that take up the most money and energy first.

Here are some things people, who we know, have done.

➤ Serve as a personal ski and snowboard guide to German tourists visiting ski resorts in the Rockies.

- Go back to college and take courses for fun.
- Trace your family tree and write a family history for the grandchildren.
- Learn how to play the fiddle and take part in bluegrass music festivals and camps.
- Build houses as a volunteer for Habitat for Humanity.
- Act as an extra in local movies.
- Volunteer with CUSO and work in a third world country.
- Take up bird watching or build unusual birdhouses and sell them.
- Volunteer with a social service agency and teach English as a Second Language to new immigrants.
- Take up kayaking and explore new lakes and rivers.
- Join a hiking group and explore new backcountry trails.
- Join a cycling club.

You need to replace work with something else that gives you satisfaction, meaning and creativity. Not that you necessarily got all of this from work.

Work your way through your list. Keeping busy doing the things that you want to do, and that give you satisfaction, will make retirement a more satisfying experience. It may be the only chance in your life to follow your dreams. Don't miss the opportunity. What are the things you want to do?

Social Connections

Have you largely ignored your family while you were working? If you answered "yes", welcome to a lonely retirement. Did you really expect anything different? Being at the peak of your game in the office comes at a high personal cost. Ask yourself these questions:

- ➤ Do you get along well with your spouse?
- ➤ How close are your relationships with your children?
- ➤ Do you regularly stay in touch with your own parents and brothers and sisters?
- ➤ Do you have any close friends?
- ➤ Have you met any interesting people lately and made new friends?

Most people need a social support system in their lives. There's always a group of colleagues to talk to, go out for coffee with, or meet for lunch when you are working. Friends and family are more important than ever when you no longer have that built-in social structure. Otherwise it is easy to feel lonely and isolated.

Don't sit at home waiting for the phone to ring. You have to take the initiative and work at developing your social connections. Do something that you enjoy. Volunteer, join a club or senior's group, or learn how to play a musical instrument. Don't wait until you retire before you get started.

Part 2:
Walking the Talk

Well done! You're making great progress. You've dealt with your fears. You know what information you need, and what you have to do—at least in theory anyway. This is the point where most retirement books end.

We all know that accepting and understanding a theory, or even common sense, for that matter, is one thing. Putting it into practice is another. That's the hard part. You are now ready for the next step. This is the nuts and bolts of retiring early.

What follows are some real life practical suggestions for ways to save up your retirement nest egg. After all, we don't want to just build up your hopes and dreams. You want your dreams to come true, don't you?

Before we go any further, we should let you know something about us. What follows aren't just academic exercises that we've read about somewhere. We practice what we preach. The techniques described in the rest of this book have allowed us to build up our own retirement nest egg.

Much of the information may seem pretty basic. That's because it is. You don't need a sophisticated computer program cranking out models of complicated investment strategies, or, for that matter, a high-priced investment consultant either. Everything you require is right at your fingertips—YOU.

The hardest part will be changing your attitude towards money and consuming. Like most of us, you probably have some deeply ingrained beliefs about money and your own self-worth that you are going to have to re-examine.

Controlling your spending is the only way we know that consistently works to save money. When you think of the alternative—giving up your dream—an attitude-readjustment doesn't seem all that bad. Perhaps it was time you started embracing conservation, rather than consumerism, anyway.

The next thing you have to do is actually do it. This may seem pretty obvious. But you have to make the effort in order to make it happen. Otherwise this is just another book you read, find interesting, and then shelve. You are no closer to reaching your dreams than before. Moreover, you're out the price of this book. Naturally, as the authors, we're grateful, but we would prefer to see you succeed.

When we began thinking about our own early retirement we read a book called *Your Money or Your Life* by Joe Dominguez and Vicki Robin. We would highly recommend this book as part of your early retirement planning. It kick-started our own retirement dreams, as it empowered us to take control of our money.

Taking back control means you have to decide what's important in your life. How successful you are depends on your motivation, and the willpower to stick to your priorities. If you insist on wasting your money on frivolous purchases, you'll never get there. Naturally, the investment industry would have you think that wealth building is the better way to go. It involves less effort and deprivation. Don't get fooled. It's easier than you think to cut back your spending.

The next four chapters contain practical advice on how to control your spending and keep track of your savings.

Chapter Twelve outlines a simple method for keeping track of your spending, which is the first step to controlling your money.

Chapter Thirteen shows how you can easily shave thousands off your budget without noticing a drop in your lifestyle.

Chapter Fourteen looks at simple everyday things you can easily do to become a conserver, rather than a consumer. You'll have the satisfaction of knowing you're an environmentally responsible citizen. The bonus is that you will save thousands of dollars every year. Isn't it satisfying to know that by doing your own small part in making this a more sustainable planet, you're also closer to realizing your own dream of retiring early?

Chapter Fifteen looks at a simple method for keeping track of your retirement savings. If you don't know when you've reached your savings goals, how will you know when to retire?

12:

Where Does Your Money Go?

So, let's get started with the real life practical stuff. This is where we separate the dreamers from the doers. You do want to retire early, don't you?

You're at home. Another hectic day is winding down. The dishes are done, the kids have finished their homework or are in bed, you've glanced through the paper and now you're wrapping up the day reading this book.

How much did you spend last month? Do you know? What did you spend it on? Go ahead. Sit down with a pencil and paper and see what you can come up with in the next fifteen minutes.

Done yet? So, how much *did* you spend last month and on what? That should be a pretty easy question to answer, shouldn't it?

The reality is it's pretty hard to remember all of your spending. If you are old enough to remember when we mostly used cash and cheques, even then you sometimes forgot to record a cheque or withdrawal in your chequebook. Now with all the ways there are to purchase things, it's even easier to forget where and how much you spent.

Mental Bookkeeping Doesn't Work

Given the number and kinds of transactions we do in a month, it isn't surprising we don't know where our money goes. Most people are too busy to do the mental bookkeeping. It would be simpler if we just paid cash or wrote a cheque. But there are so many other ways to spend money these days. Credit cards, debit cards, automatic withdrawals, prepaid cards and zero down payments make it easy to lose track of where the money goes.

Perhaps you pay the utility bill by debit card and your partner does the shopping and pays with a credit card.

Other items like the cable and Internet connection may be automatically debited from your account each month. The ease and convenience of purchasing things also makes it easier to forget that they occurred.

Some routine spending is easy to forget because we do it so often. We don't look at it as an expense. That morning coffee and muffin, or the magazine we picked up because it had an interesting article, is just part of the small indulgences we allow ourselves every day. It should be pretty obvious at this point that mental bookkeeping isn't a very effective way of keeping track of where your money goes.

We find the advice budgeting books and financial experts give isn't very useful either. You are supposed to reconstruct your expenses over the last month. In theory, you go through your chequebook, canceled cheques, debit card and ATM receipts, credit card statements, and cash register receipts.

This doesn't work because it is too impractical. How many people save the receipts for everything they buy? When was the last time you got a receipt for the latte and muffin you bought on your coffee break? Besides, who's got the time or patience to reconstruct all their previous spending?

Fortunately, there is an easier way. Don't worry. It doesn't involve budgeting. We call it the spending notebook method. We record every single cent we spend as we spend it. That is the only way we can know for sure where our money is going.

Sound like too much hassle? Not really. Just look at it this way. You work forty hours (or more) a week to earn your money. Doesn't it make sense to spend an hour or two each month to see where it's going? Think of how hard you had to work to earn it.

The spending notebook method is cheap and easy to use. All you need is a notebook and a pen or pencil.

The Spending Notebook Method

You've heard that expression, "Today is the first day of the rest of your life?" At the risk of sounding evangelical, you are about to change your life. You will be empowered to control your destiny. That's because you are now on the road to gaining control of your money.

Step 1: Record Your Spending
In order to get started, you will need the following:

- ➢ A notebook and pen. This stays at home.
- ➢ A piece of paper, an index card, or small notepad and pen. This goes with you.

Put your notebook somewhere where you can find it easily. We keep ours in the kitchen. This is where we record what we spent that day from the pieces of paper that we each carry around with us. Put your notepaper in your wallet, purse or briefcase to record tomorrow's expenses. If you have a partner, both of you have to do this.

At this point, you may be saying to yourself, "Yes, that sounds like a good idea, but I'll be logical and wait until the first day of the month to get started so my monthly record follows the calendar month. I'll get on it the first day of next month."

Yes, you are right. The calendar month is a logical period. Even so, start recording right now. Don't worry if it's already the tenth or even the twenty-third. You need to give yourself time to get in a comfortable routine that works for you. Besides, you know what happens if you procrastinate. You will never get started.

Write down what you bought and how much you paid for it. Don't be tempted to round things off. Record everything right down to the last penny. You want to get an accurate record of your spending. Don't forget that pack of gum you buy on the way to work, the two dollars you spend on a raffle ticket, the lunch you buy, or the dry cleaning you pick up on the way home. Be sure to include GST and any provincial sales tax.

What? You say this is too much work. You'll write down everything tonight when you get home. Remember how hard it is to do mental bookkeeping? The only way you'll remember is if you write down each expenditure as it occurs, or soon after.

At the end of the first day, sit down with your partner and compare your notebooks. This is no time for finger pointing and recriminations. "You spent money on what?"

At this stage, there is no guilt. Remember that this is a fact-finding mission. You just want to know where the money is going.

The numbers won't make sense just yet. At the end of one month of recording expenditures, you will need to put the numbers into categories and add them up. Don't worry about this for now.

Over the next few days, you'll start to notice a few things about yourself and your spending habits. This is the third day in a row you've bought gum in the morning and a bag of potato chips or a chocolate bar (or maybe both) in the afternoon. This is the second time in three days that your partner stopped at the store to pick up a few things for supper. Now you know why you're always going to the ATM for cash.

Continue recording expenses for the rest of the month. Be sure to add in any automatic debits such as mortgage payments, utility payments or loan payments.

At the end of the month, you will want to know two things:

> What did you buy?
> How much did you spend?

Step 2: *Organize Into Categories*

Congratulations. You've been faithfully recording your expenses for a full month. Don't forget to record non-routine but recurring expenses like vehicle, life and property insurance, vehicle licenses, and newspaper and magazine subscriptions that are usually forgotten because they occur once a year.

And then there are the irregular expenses like medications, dental, optical, home and yard maintenance, gifts, travel and school supplies. While not as precisely defined as the recurring expenses, they regularly happen nevertheless.

You now have documented evidence of the details of your spending. Think of that evening a month ago when you had trouble remembering what you spent that day, let alone the previous month.

Now it's time to group your spending into categories. This will provide information on your spending patterns. These patterns reflect your conscious and subconscious spending priorities. This is what you really want to know when you are looking at where you can change your spending, or cut back.

If you're like most people, the categories you'll first think of are the standard budget ones. These are typically food, housing, utilities, transportation, clothing, recreation/entertainment and other. On the surface, these categories seem like common sense. In reality they don't work. That's because they're too large. While they are useful in looking at the big picture, they're too general to help you understand where your money goes.

Let's take the standard general categories and see how they might be tweaked in a more meaningful way.

Food

There's nothing more basic than eating. Your monthly food bill is usually one of the biggest parts of your budget. This is especially true if you have teenagers, or eat out a lot. You want to know exactly what you spend.

As you look at your food expenses for the month, some useful subcategories suggest themselves. Grocery stores sell everything these days. You will want to break some things out. Start by looking at how much you spend on food, and use this as your first subcategory.

Next, look at what you spend on non-grocery items, like cleaning supplies, paper products, pet supplies, or shampoo and toothpaste. Set up separate subcategories for these. The first two, for example, could be included under household supplies while the third would be recorded under pets, and the last under personal supplies.

If you eat a lot of junk food, you might want a separate subcategory to record all the money you are spending on microwave popcorn, potato chips, sweets and pop.

How about eating out? Do you find yourself going out to restaurants a lot, or stopping to pick up some fast food on the way home from work? If so, set up a separate subcategory for this. You want to know how much you are spending on dining out.

You might also want a separate category for food eaten at work, if you eat out regularly. This includes lunches at work—unless you make them at home—work coffee breaks and snacks. Remember the gum?

We also include a subcategory called wine/alcohol as we make our own wine and put the costs of winemaking supplies here, as well as the occasional beer purchase.

Suddenly you realize where the food money is going. The important thing is to tailor your subcategories to reflect your own lifestyle. While you want to get an accurate idea of where your food money is going, keep your subcategories simple.

Housing

This includes your mortgage or rent payments, yard and house maintenance costs, as well as house insurance and property taxes. You probably want a separate subcategory for each of these items.

Utilities

We record our utility costs by how the bills come in. Our power, water, sewer and garbage pickup are on one bill so we record this as a lump sum. Heating costs, telephone, cable and Internet are recorded separately. Is cable a utility or entertainment expense? Again, it doesn't matter what subcategory it's in. What matters is that each transaction is recorded in a category that makes sense to you.

Transportation

What do you use to get around? Your car? Your second car? A motor home? A bicycle? Car rental? Public transportation? We match expenses with each type of transportation. For example, you might want to separate out gas, maintenance, car insurance and parking fees for each vehicle you own. Do you record work-related expenses like parking fees or bus passes here or a work expense category? The choice is yours. The bike tune-up and the LED flashing red light go in the bike category.

Entertainment

If you spend a lot of money on entertainment, it's not going to help you track your spending if you lump all your spending into one general category called entertainment. You need to break it down into subcategories. These will depend on your lifestyle and the kinds of things you like to do. How much are you spending on movies? Do you go to the theatre a lot? How about sports events and concerts? CDs and magazine purchases?

Clothing

You may want to set up a separate clothing category for each person in your household. Set it up in a way that makes sense to you, and reflects your spending patterns.

Other Categories

Other major categories include pets and education—all those school fees! Don't forget the ubiquitous 'Other'. Your categories will evolve as you see patterns of expenses emerging. The important thing is, the categories you choose need to make sense for you.

Here's a useful tip for you. If you have a computer at home set up your spending chart on a spreadsheet. We list our spending categories down the page and record the months of the year across the top of the page.

Be sure to include everything you spend money on. Include ongoing expenses like house and car insurance, utilities, loan payments, RRSP deductions and so on. There's no right or wrong way to set up your spreadsheet. The important thing is to tailor it to meet your own needs and spending habits.

The purpose of doing this is to identify your spending patterns. Don't be afraid to change your subcategories if it helps you make better sense of what you spend your money on.

We enter our spending every week or so. It's automatically added up, giving us a running total of what we have spent so far. This lets us know if our spending is out of tune with our income. Or we might find we need to cut back in one category because of more expenses that month somewhere else. It also adds up our expenses for the various categories and subcategories over the year.

Don't be surprised if you are shocked at where your money is going.

13:

A Penny Saved...

How much did you spend last month on your vehicles? On clothes? Restaurants? Entertainment? Gifts? Your spending patterns help identify your spending priorities and give you some insights into yourself. Do you really need the sixty thousand dollar SUV? The seventy-five dollar tie?

Now that you've gotten over the initial shock of where your money is going, the next step is to start thinking about your spending priorities. Are you getting the most "bang for your buck"? Or is a lot of your money going into impulse buys for things that you don't really need, or particularly even enjoy? Does the "wow" factor of your purchases justify all the money that you have spent?

There's just no getting around it. If you want to save money you have to set some priorities. Stop blowing your cash on frivolous purchases. They won't get you close to your early retirement dream.

Think of it this way. If you can reduce your budget by at least five thousand dollars a year, that's how much less you need to live on each year you are retired—and how much less you need to save. Over the course of your retirement this amount can be substantial.

It's time to start thinking of where you can cut back. You were serious about making changes in your life, right? This is where you have to start.

Painless Ways to Save

You will be surprised at how easy it is to save money. In fact, you can shave thousands of dollars off your spending every year, and not even notice a lifestyle change or feel deprived. Makes you wonder why you spent all that money in the first place, doesn't it?

Just to show you how painless it can be, let's examine the spending patterns of Caroline and Daniel, a typical middle class couple. They decided to get serious about their spending, and cut back eight thousand dollars from their budget last year. Remarkably, they haven't noticed any appreciable decline in their lifestyle.

They had some pretty expensive habits they'd gotten used to, like:

➢ Eating out frequently.
➢ Regularly going out for coffee and lunch at work.
➢ Poor grocery shopping habits.
➢ Buying clothes on impulse.
➢ Magazine and newspaper subscriptions, which they were usually too busy to read.

After making some relatively effortless changes to their lifestyle, they are now in good financial shape. The money they save is going towards paying off their debts. In fact, they plan on being debt-free in the next five years. It will be no problem to save for their early retirement after that. So what did they cut back on?

Eating Out

Caroline and Daniel noticed that most of their miscellaneous spending revolved around food and convenience. They were shocked when they added up what they were spending on these.

They were in the habit of going out for dinner with friends at least once every two weeks, usually ordered pizza on Friday nights and regularly took the family out for a fancy breakfast buffet at an expensive hotel on Sunday morning. They figured their monthly eating out costs were as follows:

Eating Out	Amount Spent
Two dinners out without the kids	$60 x 2 = $120
Babysitter	$25 x 2 = $ 50
Pizza every Friday night	$25 x 4 = $100
Breakfast buffet twice a month	$65 x 2 = $130
Total per month	$400

To their dismay, they discovered they were spending four hundred dollars a month, or a staggering $4,800 a year to eat out. Even if they cut back and eat out only half as often, they are still saving over two thousand dollars a year.

Food at Work

Caroline and Daniel have a hectic lifestyle. They seldom have time to make a homemade lunch, so usually they grab something quick at lunchtime. The following breaks down how much they spend on food at work.

Food at Work	Amount Spent
Daily coffee and muffin	$2 x 2 x 5 days/week = $20
Lunch three times per week	$5 x 2 x 3 days/week = $30
Total per month	$200

This expense added up to fifty dollars a week, or two hundred dollars a month for the two of them. Excluding holidays, they were spending a whopping two thousand dollars a year. Just for a coffee and muffin every day, and the odd bowl of soup, or fast food take-out lunch! Shocked, they started brown bagging it to work.

Now they only have the occasional lunch out. They haven't eliminated their daily coffee and muffin because this is a small indulgence they can't cut out, just yet anyway. Still, they've easily reduced their food costs at work down to one thousand dollars a year. If they cut back on their daily coffee and muffin they could reduce this expense even further.

Poor Grocery Shopping Habits

Caroline and Daniel used to be poor consumers when it came to grocery shopping. Sales flyers typically went straight into recycling. They bought whatever they wanted when they wanted, whether it was in season or a good price. They had a bad habit of loading up on convenience foods, and made several trips back and forth to the store during the week for extras. With two growing children to feed, they found their grocery bill was their biggest monthly expense.

Groceries	Amount Spent
Total per month	$900

Saving money on groceries was easy. They have learned to be better consumers, which brings them cost savings of at least $150 a month. Nowadays, when flyers arrive they carefully look them over and watch for sales. They still eat well but don't spend as much as they used to.

Now they plan their shopping trips around sales and load up on items only when they are a good price. They're not loyal to any particular store and shop wherever they can find the best deal. They've cut out convenience and junk foods.

A simple trick is to keep their pantry stocked. This way they always have something on hand to plan a quick meal around, eliminating many extra trips to the store.

Reducing their grocery bill by $150 a month means they save an average of $1,800 a year.

Impulse Clothing Buying

Caroline found she was spending a lot of money on clothes. This was easy to do as she worked downtown. Even though most items were on sale, she was still spending far more than she wanted to.

She knew her spending on clothing was out of control after a recent shopping trip. She was dismayed to find a brand new sweater that she'd completely forgotten about, buried away in the back of her closet. To her consternation, it was exactly identical to one she'd just bought at a great sale downtown.

Impulse Clothing Purchases	Amount Spent
Total per month	$300

Caroline spent an average of seventy-five dollars a week on clothes, three hundred dollars a month, or a staggering $3,600 a year! When she realized what she was spending, she stopped going to the mall at noon hour. She didn't really need most of the stuff she bought anyway. Now she goes for walks instead. The bonus is she losing weight, is more physically fit, and has reduced her clothing spending by over half, saving two thousand dollars a year.

She is more methodical about her clothing purchases now, and thinks about what she needs. When she buys something, it is good quality, and lasts longer than the cheap items she used to impulsively buy on sale.

Books, Newspaper and Magazine Subscriptions

Both Caroline and Daniel love to read. They were in the habit of buying interesting books they'd read about in the book review supplement of their newspaper. They also subscribed to several magazines and received the newspaper every day. Ironically, their hectic lifestyles meant newspapers would often go unread, magazines were quickly skimmed through, and brand new books sat on the bookshelf unread.

Cost of Reading	Amount Spent
Total per month	$100

Caroline and Daniel still love to read, but they are smarter about how they do it. They have cancelled their newspaper and magazine subscriptions, and seldom buy the latest bestsellers any more. Now they buy the paper once a week, on Saturday, and have signed up for a library card. This saves them at least one thousand dollars a year.

Adding It All Up

When you look at each item individually it doesn't seem like a big deal. So what if you have a coffee and muffin at work every day? The real surprise is when you add up all the nickel and dime stuff and find out it adds up to an astounding amount of money over the course of a year.

Much of the spending we do is mindless or routine. We don't really think about it—or just do it out of habit. A lot of our money is needlessly frittered away on things we could easily do without.

When Caroline and Daniel added up what they were saving they were astonished. Even more surprising was they barely noticed any change to their lifestyle. They easily saved the following:

Cut Back On	Amount Saved/Year
Eating out	$2,400
Coffee/lunches at work	$1,000
Groceries	$1,800
Impulse clothing purchases	$2,000
Books, magazines, newspaper subscriptions	$1,000
Total per year	$8,200

Keep in mind that these are after tax dollars. In their tax bracket, Caroline and Daniel would have had to earn around eleven thousand dollars. If they planned to keep spending this way in retirement, before shaving over eight thousand dollars off their budget, conventional retirement wisdom would dictate that they would have to have an additional $160,000 in savings, assuming a five percent return, to finance these "extras".

Obviously they weren't getting value for their money. It was easy to give these items up. They are sure they can save even more. The next set of cutbacks will be harder because they involve making lifestyle changes.

Things they have thought about doing include giving up cable TV and call display on their phones, taking the bus to work, selling a car, going camping instead of staying at fancy resorts, and spending less money at Christmas.

The list is only limited by their creativity. How far they want to continue their belt tightening exercises depends on how fast they want to reach their early retirement savings goal.

See what you can do. Keep your goal of financial freedom in mind. It will make your minor sacrifices seem easy. The best part is the realization you can retire years ahead of what conventional retirement industry wisdom would have you believe.

14:
A Shift in Attitude

Believe it or not, the biggest obstacle to saving money is your attitude. Most of us have grown up with the mentality that "more is better, and it's never enough". It's hard to stop spending, and be frugal, in a society that encourages you to demand, "What is the most that I can buy?" Can you imagine how life would be different if you asked yourself instead, "What is the least that I need, and still have a good life?"

If your spending patterns are like most North Americans, you will never realize your early retirement dreams. It's time to get your priorities straight. Are you willing to throw your dreams out that easily? You need to learn to set priorities, and stick with them. After all, what would you rather do? Have a house full of silly knickknacks and the latest electronic gadgets, or be secure in the knowledge you can quit your job anytime you want to? How much is your freedom worth to you?

So what do you have to do?

Becoming a Conserver

Most people don't give a second thought about throwing stuff away. If something is broken, why waste our time trying to fix it?

The common response is to rush out and buy a new one. The same goes for an older, but still perfectly good appliance, or something that we've simply gotten tired of. Throw it out. Upgrade to a newer model, or get it in the latest fashionable color. Landfills are filled to overflowing with our formerly prized belongings.

Charles Long, in his often entertaining and thought-provoking book, *Surviving Without A Salary*, coined the term "conserver". As Long points out, shoppers and conservers are polar opposites. That's because conservers buy something new only as a last resort. Even then, they do it reluctantly.

Long defines a conserver as someone who:

> Looks for alternative, less expensive ways to do something, rather than immediately going out and buying something new.
> Takes care of what they have to make things last longer.
> Reuses things in creative and unusual ways, getting full value out of their possessions.

Sure, you will save money. But your primary gratification is the knowledge that you are not wasting precious resources. We recently read that if everyone on earth consumed as voraciously as we do in Canada alone, we would need another two earths to sustain us with all the garbage we produce.

As part of your retire early strategy, before you buy anything new, ask yourself the following questions first:

> Do you really need it?
> Can you fix what you have instead?
> Is the cost worth it? Will you get the bang for the buck out of it?
> How often will you use it?
> Where will you store it?
> Can you borrow one instead?

Even after you decide that you really do need to buy something, try waiting twenty-four hours first. Sometimes something you thought was absolutely essential doesn't seem so urgent after all when you have had time to think about it.

The following are some simple ways to help you get off the consumer bandwagon and become a conserver instead.

Share With A Friend

Before you pull out your wallet and buy something, see if you can borrow it from a friend or neighbour first. Don't get us wrong. We're not encouraging you to become a freeloader. But sometimes it makes more sense to borrow something rather than buying a new gadget you may only use once or twice a year.

One of the best examples of sharing was with a former neighbour of ours. Walter read the local paper and then stuck it in our mailbox every night. We read it and then recycled it. This saved Walter the bother of taking a week's supply of newspapers to the recycling bin. In return, we helped him out with odd jobs around his house, as he was in his eighties.

It didn't take long to become good neighbours and friends. Walter was a widower. He never turned down the chance for a coffee and freshly baked cinnamon bun hot out of the oven.

We can still picture him sitting around our kitchen table regaling us with anecdotes, or just expounding on his philosophy of life. We had a lot of good laughs, and sorely missed Walter when we moved.

Buy Second Hand

Many people look down their noses at anything if it isn't brand new. Are you one of these people? That's a shame because you are missing out on some great bargains.

Sure, you'll have to sort through a pile of junk to find the hidden gem. But the payoff is the satisfaction in discovering something in mint condition selling for a fraction of its cost brand new.

These days, secondhand stores aren't the dark and dreary places they used to be. Frequently they're bright and airy, and have a great selection of gently used products at unbelievably low prices.

One of our best buys was a five-speed bike in excellent condition that we bought for ten dollars. It's a commuter bike for the winter so we weren't looking for all the latest bells and whistles.

We also recently bought a yoghurt-maker for three dollars. The way we saw it, if we get tired of making our own yoghurt at some point, it's not a big investment, and we won't feel guilty giving it away. Can you think of a good reason to pay more for something, particularly when there is absolutely no need to?

Another good place for bargains is garage sales, especially towards the end of the day. This is when people just want to get rid of whatever they can't sell.

Antique and estate sales are other good places to check out. Make sure you do some research before you go, though. It'd be disappointing to miss a deal because you didn't appreciate value when you saw it.

Re-Use

We find the trend to use disposable wipes for all kinds of simple household tasks disturbing. It is another example of our nonchalant attitude towards conserving and the environment.

Grocery store shelves are filled with moistened hand wipes, sterilized baby wipes, scented dusters and disposable floor mops. Believe it or not, this is a billion dollar industry. What happened to common sense? It is cheaper, not to mention more environmentally responsible, to recycle old tea towels lying around the house, or use ordinary soap and water.

With a little bit of imagination and creativity, there are a number of ways you can re-use common household items. You will feel good knowing that you are doing your part to keep landfills from filling up so rapidly with discarded junk.

Use the back of letters and school notices for grocery lists, re-use plastic food containers to store leftovers in, rinse out baggies and tin foil, use newspaper comics to wrap birthday gifts for the kids, use old cloth diapers for cleaning—the list goes on.   Go ahead. See what you can re-use around the house.

Use Public Transportation, Ride a Bike or Walk

Imagine how much money you would save if you got rid of a car and started walking or cycling to work. The added bonus is how much better you would feel.

According to the Canadian Automobile Association, the average cost of owning a car is almost eight thousand dollars a year. This includes the cost of fuel, maintenance, tires, interest expense, depreciation, insurance, license and registration fees.

Nowadays, the average family has at least two cars. Three is not that unusual. Soaring insurance premiums and hefty repair bills means that cars make up a major expense in most people's budget.

A slowly growing alternative to car ownership is car sharing. This is a concept that began in Europe and is beginning to catch on in North America. Vancouver and Toronto are two cities with car sharing co-ops. More and more people are seeing this as an economical and environmentally friendly alternative to owning a car.

When you think about it, owning a car doesn't make a lot of financial sense. The average car sits parked and unused for hours at a time. It would make a lot more sense to pay for the actual time you use a car. In that case, you could just sign one out for the time you spend running errands or driving your kids to soccer practice.

Sure, getting rid of your car is a big psychological barrier. To ease the pain, think of all the money you're saving, and take pride in the fact you're being a responsible citizen, not to mention the exercise you're getting. Certainly this option is easier if you live in an area with good public transit.

If you can't quite get yourself to get rid of all your cars, do away with one. What other incentives do you need?

Stop Buying To Impress

A lot of what we buy is to impress other people. After all, why else would you spend sixty thousand dollars on a luxury car? What if no one cared or noticed? You could just as easily pay twenty thousand dollars for something that got you from point A to point B. A car is a mode of transportation, right?

Absurd as it sounds, spending is the way most people define who they are. No one wants to settle for being average anymore.

Given our national pastime of watching TV, it's no big surprise that most people's tastes have been up-scaled. Nowadays, people expect to live how the "average" TV family lives. The problem is, Hollywood's portrayal of real family life is ludicrously removed from reality.

Young couples just starting out expect to have a large house with luxury features. In the last fifty years, the average size of the Canadian home has grown by fifty percent, even while the size of the family has shrunk.

Bigger and fancier cars are the norm. Even ordinary things we took for granted before like water, phones, or sunglasses now have an upscale version. Naturally they come with an upscale price.

It seems to be a given that the more we have, the better off we are. But does owning all this stuff really make us any happier? You wouldn't think so if you walked into any drugstore and took a close look at their shelves. They are full of remedies for depression and high blood pressure. Incidentally, these are two of the major reasons why people go to see a doctor these days.

In the long run, you will impress far more people when you walk into the boss's office, hand in your notice, and start enjoying your life of leisure years before your colleagues. They'll still be diligently toiling away at their day jobs long after you've forgotten what a timesheet is.

Poor saps. They're stressed out trying to pay off their debts for the fancy house, golf club membership, designer clothes, a new SUV, cell phones—and all the other things that outwardly validate how successful they are.

It is hard not to indulgently smile. They're frantically running with the herd, trying to keep up. You can afford to walk through life at a leisurely pace, and stop and smell the roses.

Getting Rid of Junk

It's difficult to keep track of your possessions when your garage, bureau drawers and closets are overflowing. Ironically, the classic response to clutter is to go out and buy a closet organizer to take care of the problem.

In the short run, this may seem like the answer but when you really think about it, it isn't. An organizer merely alleviates the symptom. Granted you can take pride in the fact your possessions are well ordered. But eventually you will have to go out and buy another organizer. That's because there's more empty space to fill. With all the extra shelving and drawers, there is a natural temptation to go out and buy more stuff. There are even professional organizers who will help you sort and store your stuff.

The real solution is to get rid of what you don't use or need. If your closets are jam-packed with stuff, it is time to seriously consider a garage sale. After that, you might want to mull over why you are buying so much in the first place.

The advantage of less stuff—aside from the fact your home will seem more spacious, less cluttered, and easier to clean—is that you will actually get more pleasure out of your possessions. That's because you will know what you have. You will value your possessions more, and you're more likely to take better care of them.

A good motto to live by, in fact, is to own just a few fine things. Pack up all the rest. This includes things like ornaments, dishes, books, clothing, furniture or anything else you bought over the years, but think you really don't need. Put these items into boxes. Then put the boxes into storage. Give yourself about six months. If you don't miss the items that you packed—and you probably won't—sell or donate them. We guarantee that you will feel lighter, without having gone on a diet.

Once you've de-cluttered and edited your life of those things that are extraneous, you'll wonder why you didn't do it sooner.

Valuing Frugality

It is only fair to warn you. We are not going to mislead you and say it will be easy to get off the consumer bandwagon. The reality is that our society doesn't value frugality.

Let's be honest here. What words come to mind when you think of frugal? Tightwad? Cheapskate? Skinflint? Not exactly flattering, right? Somehow, frugality has gotten an undeservedly bad reputation.

In reality, frugal people should be held up as role models. Their everyday actions promote sustainability and a greener environment. Frugality is much more than the stereotype of the miserly old man next door hanging his teabags out to dry so he can re-use them, especially when he's got company coming.

We would even venture to say a frugal person is a better citizen, as they care about their community. They value their possessions, and take care of what they have. They are not needlessly wasteful.

By contrast, a spendthrift doesn't have a clue what they own. They are always rushing off to buy the next big thing. They are never happy with what they have because there is always something newer and fancier to buy.

We suspect their shopping addiction is a quick fix to fill a void in their lives.

Have you ever thought it's peculiar how we're so indulgent towards spendthrifts? By now you know what lies ahead. They'll be working to pay off their debts long after you've retired.

15:
Keeping Track of Retirement Savings

You're at home. Another hectic day is winding down. The dishes are done. The kids have finished their homework or are in bed. You've glanced through the paper. Maybe you're starting to already think about work tomorrow.

If this sounds familiar, you're a sharp reader. Those were the opening lines to Chapter Twelve, *Where Does Your Money Go?* We talked about the notebook method for tracking your spending. Now we're going to tell you about a method for tracking your savings. It stands to reason that if you don't know how much you money you have saved, how will you know when you can retire?

Most people have at least one RRSP. In fact, it's not uncommon for people to have six or seven RRSPs at different financial institutions.

How many RRSPs do you have? Your RRSPs may consist of a combination of GICs, money market accounts, mutual funds, bonds and equities. How much are they worth? If you have some GICs or bonds, when are they maturing? How many mutual funds do you have? How many different bank accounts do you have and where?

If you're like most people, you may have a general idea of what you have in the way of savings. The problem is with the specifics. Not many people do all their banking and investing with one institution. Your savings may be dispersed in banks, credit unions, insurance companies, investment firms and mutual fund companies.

Who can keep track of all that? Before you can start drawing on your income sources, you need to know where they are, and how much you have.

The Savings Notebook Method

If you've been faithfully saving all those financial statements you regularly get, you're off to a good start. What you need to do now is to summarize all that information onto a couple of pages. The easiest way to do this is to get on the computer and start listing out each item. The reason you want to do this on a computer is so you can easily make updates. Record your savings in two sections.

Section One

This is a listing of accounts by person. It lists:

> * All the various accounts you have.
> * What financial institution they're held at.
> * The purchase value.
> * The rate of return.
> * When they mature, if applicable.

A sample format is shown on the next page.

Section 1: Listing of Accounts and Investments

List of Accounts	Interest Rate	Date Updated Maturity
Jennifer		
Royal Bank RRSP Account		
$20,000 Canada Bond	4.9%	Dec 1, 2007
$10,000 BC Bond	5.134%	Aug 3, 2007
$6,900 Canada Strip Bond	4.158%	June 8, 2009
CIBC RRSP Account		
$6,000Canada Strip Bonds	6.56%	June 1, 2011
$16,000 5-Year GIC	2%+3%+4%+5%+7.5%	Feb 8, 2007
Etc.		
Calvin		
Royal Bank RRSP Account		
$5,000 Canada Bond	7.25%	June 1, 2007
$20,000 Canada Bond	5.5%+5.7%+5.9%	Nov 1, 2010
Etc.		

Section One changes as your portfolio changes. The listing will give you a quick overview of what you have and where it is.

Section Two

This section describes each asset in greater detail:

> - What you paid for it.
> - The yield.
> - Its current market value.
> - When it matures.

A sample format is shown below.

Section 2: Detailed Listing of Savings/Investments

Type of Investment	Date Updated Market Value
Jennifer	
Royal Bank RRSP Account	
Government of Canada Bonds	
$20,000 worth maturing December 1, 2007	
4.9% yield	
Current Market Value	$22,008
Government of B.C. Bonds	
$10,000 worth maturing August 23, 2007	
5.134% yield	
Current Market Value	$11,620
Etc.	
Total Value of Jennifer's RRSPs	$XXXX
Calvin	
Royal Bank RRSP Account	
Government of Canada Bonds	
$5,000 worth maturing June 1, 2007	
7.25% yield	
Current Market Value	$6,615
Etc.	
Total Value of Calvin's RRSPs	$XXXX
Grand Total	$XXXX

This section gets updated whenever a financial statement arrives in the mail. Add up the current or market values for each person and the grand total. This is your retirement bankbook. We have this set up in Excel. The totals are automatically added up, which simplifies the amount of work we have to do.

You now have a detailed picture of your savings and how they are doing. You will know when investments are maturing and when you need to take action. As an added bonus, you also have a record of where everything is. If you or your partner were to suddenly pass away, the survivor would know what assets there are, and where they are located.

This format works for us. Feel free to experiment and come up with a system that works for you.

Watch Your Money Grow

A great morale booster is to chart your savings on a large piece of paper. Prominently display this somewhere where you can easily see it, such as a wall in your home office. Your graph could be much like the thermometer used for United Way campaigns, with zero at the bottom and your target savings amount at the top.

Keep coloring your chart in until you reach your savings goal. There is an immense feeling of accomplishment watching your money grow knowing your freedom is close at hand.

16:

So, What are You Going to Do?

So what *are* you going to do? The established option most people choose—we suspect more by default than anything else—is to stick with the experts. In that case anticipate years of time-consuming commutes, endless mind-numbing meetings, and long, demanding hours at the office still lying ahead.

But then, did you expect anything different? That's the million-dollar price of retirement. If you're lucky, you might be able to slow down and abandon the rat race one day when you finally reach your savings goal, or you qualify for your full pension. Your only worry then is to hope that the kids don't squander the money on high-priced lawyers as they fight over the large inheritance you plan to leave them. Or the government doesn't take it all.

Or else you can take a different approach. Get off the treadmill and start enjoying life now. Happiness isn't something you can buy. It comes from intangibles—family and friends, good health, the time to do the things you have a passion for.

Many people who have successfully retired early will tell you that early retirement is nowhere near as hard as it sounds. They've discovered that there is no need to focus on wealth building. The trick is to cut your spending instead. Keep your expectations modest. Conspicuous consumption is a blind alley in the pursuit of happiness, anyway, and won't make up for missing the boat on your dreams.

The following are things everyone can do. All it takes is some commitment on your part, and a willingness to live within your means.

> Keep your living costs low.
> Minimize debt.
> Pay off your house.
> Save a modest amount of money. Most middle class Canadians can comfortably live on thirty percent to fifty percent of what they grossed during their working years.

- Put money into RESPs for your children, so they are self-supporting when you retire.
- Think about your tax situation. Plan your income to avoid high tax rates or clawbacks on your benefits.
- Don't worry about an inheritance for the kids. If you want to help them out, do it now.
- Think about what you want to do. Start making a list so you have something you can hardly wait to get started doing to keep you motivated.
- Look after your health. Don't skimp on going to the gym, or out for a walk, because you have to catch up on paperwork at the office. Your health is too important to neglect or take for granted.
- Value your family and friends. Don't make the mistake of abandoning them for the office.

If you want to change your life you can. It's your choice. There's no reason why most middle class Canadians can't retire early if they take the time to plan ahead.

So what's your choice? Do you want to continue working hard, and die rich? Or do you want to start enjoying life now? The answer seems pretty obvious, doesn't it?

Perhaps we'll see you out for a leisurely stroll with your dog, taking a watercolor class, skiing, kayaking, relaxing with friends at an outdoor cafe, or enjoying the sights in South America on a beautiful weekday morning sometime in the near future.

The Final Word is Yours

If you have any comments, retirement tips, stories or suggestions for improvement, we'd love to hear from you.

You can reach us at: FinePrintPress@interbaun.com

Or, if you prefer to write:

FinePrintPress
Box 105, 14035-105 Avenue
Edmonton, Alberta
T5N 0Z1

Check your local bookstore or order here.

Order Form

Please send me _____ copies of **Why Swim With the Sharks?** for $24.95 each plus $3.00 each for shipping and handling. Payment must accompany orders.

Name_____

Street_____

City_____

Province_____Postal Code_____

Amount Enclosed_____

Make your cheque payable and return to:
FinePrintPress
Box 53105, 14035-105 Avenue
Edmonton, Alberta
T5N 0Z1